What Would You Do If You Were Me?

A Testimony of Survival in Prison

RAYLAN GILFORD

NEWMAN SPRINGS PUBLISHING
320 Broad Street
Red Bank, NJ 07701

First originally published by Newman Springs Publishing 2021

ISBN 978-1-63692-364-2 (Paperback)
ISBN 978-1-63692-365-9 (Digital)

Printed in the United States of America

Contents

Acknowledgments

This book is dedicated to the realest man I have ever known, Devon Raymone Henderson, "My Brother" (smile). Because of you, I no longer fear life or death, and you know what I'm talking about.

I'm sorry that I failed as your big brother. But rest assured, your kids are now my kids and I got 'em. I miss you so much Gully and I can't wait to see you again. Marshmallow Krispies!

Incarceration Timeline

July 1994. Chicago Cook County Jail: maximum security; division 9 (a little over nine months).

May 1995. Joliet Correctional Center: maximum security (three years, four months).

September 1998. Menard Correctional Center: maximum security (eight years, five months).

February 2007. Western Illinois Correctional Center: medium-maximum security (four years, eleven months).

January 2012. Danville Correctional Center: medium security (until present).

Introduction

I am forty-five years of age. I have been incarcerated for twenty-six years straight within the Illinois Department of Corrections. Over the years of this perilous, laughable, and oftentimes fucked-up journey, one thing has remained constant: *the fear.*

In one form or another, *fear* has ruled every aspect of my penal existence. Housed within the back of my mind are daily fears, such as contaminated water, bacteria-infected food, yard dismissal, visit restrictions, commissary denial, lost mail, segregation, and cancelled phone privileges. Also the fear of my girl moving on with another man, ailing relatives, sick children, and the loss of loved ones ceaselessly haunt my entire psyche. But the fear of being extorted, robbed, beat up, stabbed, shot, raped, gang raped, disfigured, maimed, paralyzed, or even killed reign supreme. That is too much pressure for a city of men to endure, let alone one man for multiple decades.

By raising my penitentiary IQ, I have found positive ways of accepting and dealing with said fears. But there is one fear that I have been unable to find a remedy for, and that is the terrorizing fear I feel each and every time I am housed with a new cellmate.

I would like for you to step into my shoes for a minute. Imagine being locked in a ten-by-seven-foot cell with a complete stranger. Now add on the fact that this person is a convicted felon as well. Upon introduction, if there is one, guilt or innocence is not in question. More pressing and alarming factors roll through your mind, such as: is he a murderer, a rapist, or a pedophile? Can we coexist in this small space? Is he mentally ill or physically disabled? Does he have seizures? Does he wash his hands and ass? Is he violent, territorial, argumentative, or confrontational? Is he a homosexual, a bootie bandit, or a thief? Will he do ungodly things to my opened food and personal hygiene items when I am not in the cell? Will he purposely break my $206.19 Clear Tunes fourteen-inch flat-screen television, $46.00 Sony Walkman, or $26.08 Lasko Whirlwind twelve-inch fan while I am in school? Does he have bedbugs, cooties, or scabies? Does he have hepatitis A, B, or C; tuberculosis; or HIV/AIDS? Will he physically attack me while I am awake? And, most frightening of all, will he assault me while I am sound asleep?

Over the twenty-six years of my incarceration, I have had over a thousand different cellmates. *What Would You Do If You Were Me? A Testimony of Survival in Prison* is a collage of five of the most evil, crazy, diabolical, and nasty inmates that I have had the nonpleasure of being housed with throughout the last two decades. Maybe I can heal myself of all this trauma by sharing these stories with you. Or at the very least I can stop some little boy or girl from coming to prison. PARENTAL DISCRETION IS ADVISED.

CHAPTER 1

The Toenail Man

When I was housed at Western Illinois Correctional Center—house 4, D wing, upper tier—a middle-aged, semi-overweight, scruffy-looking White man with a small head and beady eyes opened the cell door and proceeded to introduce himself. This was a great start because that signified to me that he had manners. In kind, I said hello, stated my name, and gave him some dap. Then I helped him move his personal property into our cell. As he arranged his TV and other items upon the upper shelf, we began to chitchat.

"Man, it's pretty clean up here," he said as he rubbed his hand across the shelf.

"Yeah, I wipe down everything at least once a week," I responded as I slid back on the bottom bunk to give him as much room as possible to situate his things.

He looked at me in a weird way, smiled, and said, "*Oh*, I ain't got to do nothing then, huh?"

"I don't care whether you clean up or not. All I ask is that you take a shower every day, 'cause it's too hot to be smelling another man." ·

"I take a shower every two or three days."

I laughed out loud because I thought he was joking, but when I looked into his eyes, I realized that he was as serious as a constipated man with hemorrhoids trying to take a shit. Such a great beginning just took a sharp turn for the worst. I shook my head in dismay and thought to myself, *Here we go again.*

Maya Angelou once said, "When people show you who they are, believe them." And true to his words, this funky motherfucker would go two, and oftentimes three, whole days without washing his ass. Two men sweating in a box in summertime with the humidity high as ever, and he still wouldn't take a shower. God help me!

After about three weeks of my nostrils burning, I tried to talk to him about his unconventional bathing routine.

"Cellie, can I holler at you for a minute?"

"Yeah."

"I can wait until your show go off."

"Go ahead, I saw this episode already."

"I'm not trying to be disrespectful or offend you in any type of way, but you got an odor coming off your body."

"Yeah I know. I'm going to take a shower today," he responded flippantly.

I maintained my composure and continued.

"I'm trying to talk to you about the days that you don't take a shower. The smell that's coming off your body right now might not be as strong the day after you shower, but on day two and especially day three, you stank man."

"I don't have soap like you to take showers every day."

"I'll give you a bar of soap whenever you run out. All you got to do is let me know."

"I don't need no handouts from you!" he screamed out loud.

"It ain't about that. You making my bit hard when I got to keep smelling your funky ass!" I responded in a like tone.

"I don't take showers every day. I didn't do it at home, and I'm definitely not going to do it in prison for you!"

"And that's *that?*"

"*Yeah!*"

He put his headphones on and went right back to watching an already-seen television program. I ain't going to lie; I was madder than Mean Joe Green and Mr. T when he pities a fool. Here I am trying to communicate and coexist with this shit bag, and he goin' loud-talk me and then go back to watching a rerun like *fuck what I'm talking about.* It took all the strength that my manhood could muster to stay in control and keep my hands to myself. Honestly, he didn't know how close he came to being snatched up out that top bunk and punched in his fucking mouth.

I chose to turn down because I wasn't trying to go back behind the wall to Menard Correctional Center maximum security prison. Why? Western Illinois Correctional Center is a medium-maximum security prison, which means quite a few things: only locked gates and fences surround me now, and I have a limited view of the outside world. No more bars or a thirty-foot-high gravel wall is used to separate me from semimainstream America like in Menard. Shit, I could write a whole 'nother book about the debilitating psychological effects of those railroad iron bars and that kryptonite concrete wall. So let's just move on.

Medium-maximum security also means fewer restrictions and more privileges. For example, the opportunity to take a shower every day as opposed to showering only two times a week in Menard's maximum-security prison. Yeah, that's hard time for real! Living under those conditions for years, I ain't ashamed to admit that I kept a jock itch when I was behind the wall. Most importantly, Western Illinois Correctional Center is a three-and-a-half to four-hour drive from Chicago, and Menard is a seven-and-a-half to eight-hour ride from the city. My mom was real sick around this time. She contracted pulmonary fibrosis, which is an infectious respiratory disease, so whenever her health permitted and she got a hold of a couple of extra dollars, she would come and visit me. Being the mama's boy that I am, I wanted to do everything in my power to make her drive as stress-free as possible, even if that meant I had to smell a sweaty dick, bootie, and balls with the funk of a three-hundred-pound Tarzan sprinkled on top.

Real talk: to combat his BO, I stockpiled fabric softeners from the inmate commissary. I would spaciously tape four of them at the bottom of the top bunk and swap out those wisps of freshness about every three days. Fabric softeners cost $2.38 with twenty-five sheets to a box. For an indigent man in prison like myself, that was a helluva high price to pay for the smell of normalcy. Regretfully, I was forced to go without some of my favorite comfort snacks: Snickers, Skittles, and Cherry Cokes. Self-denial and being the bigger man were my only options. If I talked to the police about moving because of stank-man hygiene issues, I'd be viewed as weak by the inmate population and maybe even labeled a stool pigeon. The prison walls have ears. From my incarcerated experience, I've found that men gossip just as much as women, if not more. So you can best believe that damn near everybody in the prison has heard about a White boy loud-talking me almost as fast as the speed of light.

Please don't be offended by the term "White boy." I knew he was a man. I'm just trying to expose you to the inner workings of the prison mind, penitentiary language, and the culture of incarceration. So be warned, the narratives are going to be graphic, politically incorrect, and verbally abusive from here on out. So don't expect any more apologies from me. You asked for this if you continue to read on, so enjoy the ride!

If I threatened him and/or we got to fighting in that little-ass cage, I'd be thrown into segregation. For me, confinement within confinement would hurt worst of all. If my mom came to visit, I wouldn't be able to hug her or hold her hands due to the five-inch-thick *Star Trek* Plexiglas used to punish and separate segregation inmates from their family members, loved ones, and friends. So it was a lose-lose situation—you feel me?

I decided to put him on "No Talk," meaning I ain't saying shit to him outside of the words "Excuse me" when I passed him by in that wee-man cell. Communication is the cornerstone to any living arrangement, even more so in prison because you don't have any-where to go. So once communication was thrown out the window, all that was left in a two-man, pantry-sized room with a bunk bed, toilet, and sink was hella tension, anger, and a lot of resentment. I lived with this shitty-bootie dude for seven months straight with a smile on my face. Granted it was the Joker smile but a smile none-theless. And it was all because my mom said, "Be patient baby boy, I'm on my way."

Then finally, after two hundred and fourteen days of being trapped in an overused Porta Potty, my mom came to see me, Alhamdulillah! Renewed and reinvigorated by the love that only a mother can give, I returned to that musty-ass cell stronger than ever with a new sense of purpose. I thought to myself while closing the door behind me, *I don't care what this nasty motherfucker smell like. I'm a mind my business and keep hanging those fabric softeners because mom said she'd be back real soon.*

Two weeks passed before the loftiness of those thoughts deflated. One Sunday morning, I began cleaning the cell as usual. First, I folded back my mattress and placed both of our property boxes on the clear end of the bottom bunk. A property box is a four-foot-long, three-foot-wide, one-foot-high plastic container assigned to an inmate upon entry into a facility. It is used to store personal items such as clothes, books, food, etcetera.

Next, I stacked our legal boxes on top of the property boxes. A legal box is the same height but about a third the size of a property box. It is called a legal box because we are only allowed to store legal material inside. Anything other than court papers found in that space will be confiscated by a correctional officer. Plainly put, the area of my entire estate consists of a bottom dresser drawer and a top left-handed sock drawer filled with ants. Now, who said crime doesn't pay?

It's customary—better yet, wise—to wipe down the floor with a damp rag before you soap it up to remove all the dust particles and shed man hair. So after I placed everything that was on the ground upon the bottom bunk, I wet a face towel with warm water, got on my hands and knees by the door, and proceeded to dust-mop the entire cell. Rag in hand, left to right I went with *The Miseducation of Lauryn Hill* playing softly in the background. Yeah, I was in my element. After about three Daniel-san (the original Karate Kid) wax-ons and wax-offs, I abruptly stopped at the toilet area when something pricked the palm of my right hand.

"What the *fuck?*" I said out loud to no one in particular as I examined my hand.

When I realized no skin had been broken, I began to relax. Then I flipped over the towel, raised it up, and held it over the toilet, and a toenail fell into the water. I didn't trip at that time. I just figured my cellie clipped his toenails and when he went to dispose of them in the toilet, one got away from him. So I soaped my rag up, damped it down again, and continued on. Two wax-ons and wax-offs later, I felt something sharp again under the palm of my wiping hand.

Come on now, this can't be, I said in my head.

I turned the rag over, and there's a fucking toenail. I thought to myself, *I know this nasty ass nigga ain't throwing his toenails around this cell after he clipped 'em off. Naw, he ain't that crazy.*

So I shook that bad boy off the towel into the toilet and kept going. When I got to the last corner of the cell, guess what I saw? *A goddamn toenail!* Here it is this White nigga too trifling to wash his own ass on a regular basis and too lazy to clean up, and now on top of all that he was throwing his gargoyle talons around the room. I was madder than a fat, White, Southern, racist-ass highway patrolman who just caught his nineteen-year-old daughter naked in his bed, getting double-teamed by a Black panther and an illegal Mexican immigrant. I turned off my radio, grabbed that last toenail, snatched his headphone cord from his TV, and said, "What the fuck is *this?*" as I displayed the toenail in the middle of the rag. Not really needing an answer, I mugged up and continued.

"Man, I know you ain't clipping your toenails and just throwing 'em around this cell!"

His beady little eyes got as big as a couple of freshly minted BOE dollars.

"Rasheed, I swear I ain't do that!"

"Well how did three toenails get on the floor, then?"

"I probably drug them in on the bottom of my shower shoes from the shower."

"Who in the fuck is clipping they toenails naked in a prison shower?"

"I swear Rasheed, I drug 'em in."

His lies only infuriated me more, but I calmed down because my mom said she'd be back real soon. I'd also learnt from life experience that people lie for one of three reasons. One, they owe you money. Two, they blow things up bigger than what they truly are for attention or because of low self-esteem. Or three, they're scared for some reason. I looked in this man face, and number three was written all over it. So I dumped the final toenail in the toilet, channeled my anger, and cleaned the cell floor with the vengeance of eighteen disciplined samurais. After the tiles dried, I placed the property and legal boxes back in their designated areas, changed rags, and then proceeded to wipe down the shelves where our electronics and miscellaneous items were placed.

The top wood-paneled shelf is about four feet long and two feet wide, stationed six feet high on the wall directly across from the bunk bed. From a logistical standpoint, whether I sat on the top bunk or lay back to rest my head upon a piss-stained pillow, I'd be able to view my fourteen-inch television comfortably, and my fan would hit me just right. The middle shelf positioned about two feet down is the same length and width as the top one. The third and final shelf is about one third the size of the other two. Then there is a two-by-two-feet shelf/desk that can be used for drawing and writing letters. But more times than not, this shelf/desk is where the bottom bunk occupant places his TV and fan.

Each cell contained a plastic chair, and I stepped upon it to wipe down the top shelf where my cellmate keeps his electronic items. I raised his fan and wiped under it, and as I moved the damp towel towards his TV, guess what I saw? You bet your sweet ass it was *another motherfucking toenail!* This time around, after snatching his headphone cord from the television, I jumped off the chair and yelled with destruction in my eyes, "How this toenail get up here then? I'm finna beat your bitch ass!"

I balled up my fist and cocked my right hand back, anxious to embed my knuckles inside the warm and inviting softness of his pale-skinned face.

"Rasheed, nooo!" he screamed as he curled into a funk ball and wrapped his arms around his head and face.

The screech was so loud that he snapped me out of a disturbingly violent and demonic trance.

"Please Rasheed, I'll move tomorrow, don't do it!"

He squealed over and over with his eyes closed. Seeing that I was in full control, I turned down physically, but at the same time I was still pissed. I thought to myself, *This all I had to do to get this piece of shit up outta here! Fuck that. This White nigga punished me for seven months. I gotta get my lick back.* So I went on a revenge-filled rant and verbally chastised him until my head starting hurting.

"Your bitch ass, you don't wanna wash your ass, and on top of that you gone throw toenails around this bitch like I'm that nigga to fuck with? Okay, you better stay in the bunk all day and *all* mother-fucking night. If you get off that top bunk, I'm a beat your ass. You bet not even fart 'cause I'm a take that as an act of aggression and stomp your motherfucking ears together. I'm tired of your shit! If you even cough, I'm a knock your ass out!"

"Sheed, man, calm down!" one of my homies yelled from next door.

"Fuck that man, I'm tired of this nasty-ass White boy. You bet not even breathe normal in this bitch—"

And on I went until my head started pounding. Yeah y'all, I went a little crazy. But in my defense, that was months of built-up pressure from living with a vagabond toppled with hurtful flashbacks of my fifty dollars' worth of Skittles going down the drain for fabric softeners.

After I calmed down and came back to my senses, it was a long night until morning 'cause I could not soundly sleep after threating this man's life. By that same token, it was an even longer night for him because he went about twenty hours without food, water, sound, and restroom breaks. Add to this, he also had to worry about me jumping up in the middle of the night and pounding him out for all the olfactory trauma that he had willingly put me through.

Monday morning, he talked to his culinary arts teacher, and she got him moved that same day.

What would you do if you were me?

CHAPTER 2

The Sexual Deviant

Back in 2004–2005-ish, I was placed in the East House on gallery 7 cell 720 at Menard Correctional Center. Around that time, Menard held about three thousand inmates and was divided into four separate housing units. You had the North House for low aggression and protective custody (PC) inmates. The South House was where all the inmates with prison jobs lived. The East House was where the high-aggression inmates/convicts rest their heads, and the West House held the extremely high aggression inmates/convicts. The term *aggression* is code for violent, unruly, crazy, dangerous, uncontrollable, and/or psychotic escape risks.

Throughout the many years of my life spent at Menard Correctional Center, I lived in all four houses at one point in time or another. Before the sexual deviant walked into my life, I had been staying in the East House for at least two years. How did I land there? I was involved in a series of fistfights adhering to the unwritten penitentiary version of the "Stand Your Ground" law. Basically, I had a choice: fuck or fight, and I chose the latter of the two because I have never been a fan of correctional sex. Naw, I'm just playing; it wasn't nothing that serious. I just had to stomp a few niggas out over regular old prison shit.

The sound of metal upon metal awoke me from a restful sleep. I rubbed my eyes and squinted toward the noise. The sound was Officer Dickface taking the cell door off deadlock. He keyed the second lock, then snatched the iron-barred door open with his free hand. You best believe the American public is safer than safe from Menard Correctional Center prisoners because every single cell door has not only a regular ironman lock but a deadbolt lock on top of that one, and I'm not even counting the various other cast-iron locked doors one would have to melt down and go through just to get a whiff of fresh air.

Picture this: every night after chow, an officer hastily walks down the gallery slamming each individual iron cell door shut, locking in the occupants. Boom! *Boom! Boom!* Boom! *Boom!* The closer the officer comes to your cell the louder the boom gets. Then around 6:00 p.m., the same officer goes to every cell door and deadbolts an already-locked door. Click! *Click! Click!* Click! *Click!* Double bubble baby.

The East House is like a five-story warehouse that's made of nothing but ronin iron and soulless concrete. So you know there is a helluva echo. The East House is chopped up into two sections with five levels on each side, numbered 1 to 10. One level contains twenty-five two-man cages, and every individual cage door has to be slammed shut and deadlocked. Can you imagine the echoing sounds of 250 cell doors being slammed shut and deadlocked throughout the building every single night? Boom! *Boom!* Boom! Then click! *Click!* Click! Night after night, *every goddamn night.*

Now for those of you who may be wondering why it's so hard for us to be rehabilitated, wonder no more, because those sounds are just one of the many psychological traumas that I'm going to expose throughout the course of this story. It's 2021, fourteen years later, and I can still hear that fucking noise in my head. Often I awake from peaceful sleep and blissful wet dreams because of those traumatizing teeth-grinding sounds.

Well, anyway. Officer Dickface pulled the cell door open, and in came my new roomie. I sat up straight on the top bunk and watched him as he pushed all his property in at once. His legal box and thirteen-inch color TV was on top of his property box and his mattress was rolled up and planted on top of everything else. Officer Dickface slammed the door shut behind my new cellmate. *Boom!* Then he said, "You be good now Gilford."

I responded, "I ain't got no choice. You got an officer standing over there on the catwalk with a fully loaded carbine."

Officer Dickface threw his dick-shaped head back and laughed as he walked away.

Oh, I forgot to mention, every floor gallery is about five feet wide with floor-to-ceiling steel bars welded in for a balcony. The barred terrace has multiple functions, but only three stand out in my mind:

1. It's a safety measure instilled to prevent inmates and officers alike from being tossed off the higher decks.
2. It's a constant reminder that a nigga is locked up for real, for real. Even if you tried to look past your cell bars for some solace, it's not goin' to work, 'cause you ain't gonna see nothing but more prison bars.
3. It—and I believe this is the most significant reason—keeps us inmates/convicts from getting on the "catwalk" where all the murder weapons are held.

The catwalk is like a grated gallery made of nothing but metal and steel. It's located inside the building on the opposite wall from the cells about thirty feet away, welded in between the third and fourth floors, and it circles around the entire East House. It's called the catwalk because you have an officer on each side of the building walking back and forth watching and stalking their prey like an undomesticated cat who's ready to pounce the instant an institutional infraction is made. These correctional officers are armed with various high-grade military weaponry such as M16s, M14s, .30 ought 06s, carbines, twelve-gauge shotguns, etcetera.

Beanbags, what the fuck is that? All the ammo here is live. If you're lucky, you'll get a warning shot aimed at the sporadically placed shot boxes along the top galley wall. A shot box is a three-foot-long-by-three-feet-wide wooden box that's about six inches thick. No doubt it's filled with bulletproof vest material because it's used to catch hold of any discharged slugs. Painted on the outside of a shot box is a three-inch outer black circle with a handball-sized bloody-red bull's-eye in the middle. Now, if you're not so lucky, the first warning shot will be at the crowd where the disturbance is taking place, and if you got buzzard luck, you could be uninvolved with the ruckus and still get shot by a poorly trained and/or scary-ass correctional officer.

The most terrorizing and disheartening part about the last two scenarios is the mere fact that there will be a coverup. A second shot will be fired into the shot box and/or the incident report will be written as if you were heavily involved in the bullshit when in reality you're innocent. Welcome to the land of a righteous shooting and/or another justifiable homicide! So why put your hands up? In here, they gonna shoot anyway.

Answer this: how can we get the truth out? Who in their right mind is going to believe convicted felons? We're all liars and thieves, the perfect alibi. But I digress.

I jumped out of my bunk, wet my face towel, and proceeded to wipe the crust from my eyes. When I turned around from the sink, a tall, skinny, six-footish, dark skinned, Black man with an average-size head and long plaited hair stood before me.

"What's up man? My name's Rasheed," I said, breaking the silence with my early-morning dog's breath.

"They call me X-Man."

"Like the superhero?"

"Naw, 'cause I ain't got no problem with X'ing you out if you cross that line."

I was taken aback by that statement because I wasn't sure if this nigga was speaking in general or he just threatened my life. So I mugged up a little and responded in like tone.

"Yeah, lines are good. They keep everything in order."

Then I turned back around and began brushing my teeth while X-Man arranged his things.

"What time we go to chow over here?" he asked.

I made him wait until I was completely finished with my oral routine before I responded. I even gargled a few times with warm water just to prolong the affair.

"Between nine and ten o'clock," I responded as if I was annoyed. Then I proceeded to get dressed.

"Damn, that's way too early. We go about eleven o'clock in the West House."

I guess that was his own little way of telling me that he just came from the most dangerous housing unit in Menard. So I would assume that he was some type of badass. This revelation didn't move me because I lived in the West House before. It was just another part of the joint to me. I'm more dangerous than two of the most dangerous motherfuckers when my life is on the line.

"Is that so," I dryly retorted.

Quick side note: What we are doing right now is playing psychological cell games. We're trying to determine who is going to rule who in this super tiny cell. Personally, I prefer that we view each other as equals and just get along in this scanty space. But not everyone in prison is as progressively minded as I. So on we went because I refuse to let any man stand on me.

"Why you on the top bunk instead of the bottom?" he asked.

"I got a seminice view of the Mississippi River up there."

"Damn, let's switch!"

"Naw, I'm straight."

"I'll take your top bunk," he said of a surety like I'm a bitch or something.

In that instant, I had made up my mind to smash him out and go back to seg for at least thirty days for such blatant disrespect. But when I looked his way with the mask of a Skynet Terminator, he had a big Kool-Aid smile on his face. And right then and there, I was convinced to believe that I had been the only one tripping. Earlier, when he shared the explanation of his name, he hadn't threatened my life; he was just speaking about his name in general, and everything negatively stated from then on out was only happening in my head. And there I was about to destroy this man's face for no reason at all. Damn, Menard really fucked me up. So anyway, I relaxed, smiled back, and let the real me take control.

"You take my bunk, you better be ready to take a Bruce Lee ass-whoopin' that come with it." And we laughed together. I exhaled and thought in my mind, *We might be all right in this bitch.*

He had surprisingly exceptional cell etiquette. When he passed gas, he would sit on the toilet and flush it down. He took showers on shower day, bird-bathed on the other days, washed his hands after using the restroom facility, and cleaned up behind himself. We watched many of the same programs, like *Buffy the Vampire Slayer* and *Stargate Atlantis*. So now I had someone to joke and converse with about the comedic and dramatic events that took place on my favorite television shows. He even knew how to create his own space in a spaceless area. So when he fell back and worked on his drawings, I would listen to my music or disappear for many hours inside the wonderful land of romance, courtesy of Ms. Danielle Steel herself. Days turned to weeks, and weeks developed into months; before I knew it, a whole year had flown by. Outside of a few spatial bumps here and there, we got along just fine.

Side note: Behind the wall, it's very disrespectful to ask a man what he's locked up for and/or how much time he has to do. Being a Curious George about that topic is a surefire way to get your head busted or stabbed in the mouth. But if someone opens the door and willingly shares that information, then it's okay to walk right on in and ask away.

One night, X-Man was venting about a confrontation he had earlier in the day with another convict. I refused to advise him on how he should proceed. All I was willing to do was be a nonjudgmental sounding board for him. No matter how bad I wanted to solve this simple problem he faced, I had to obey the First Rule of Incarceration: "Mind your own fucking business." So for me to voice an opinion in any capacity would be in total violation of rule one, increasing the odds of me being seriously injured or killed. Fuck him; I gotta make it home safe.

Anyway, in the midst of his clamoring, he said, "I got eighty-five years to do. That's too much time to be dealing with this bullshit."

My ears stood up like a German shepherd in heat, and as he wound down he asked a question that I was unwilling to answer.

"What you think I should do, man?"

"I don't know. That's a tough one there."

"What would you do if you was in my position?"

Knowing what he was alluding to, I changed the whole conversation around.

"You got eighty-five years for what?" I asked.

"A murder," he stated matter-of-factly, and then started all over again from the beginning of that weak-ass dilemma.

I heard him speaking the second time around but I wasn't actively listening like I was the first time. Honestly, I was stuck on that "eighty-five years for a murder" statement. I thought to myself, *This nigga lying. Murder only carry twenty to sixty years. He done some other shit.* So I removed from my eyes those "see only the good" baby-blue contact lenses and put on my Southside Chi-Town bifocals.

I began to notice a lot of little weird shit he would do around the cell that at first went unnoticed. For instance, I recognized that whenever I would get out the top bunk to grab a snack, take a piss, or whatever, he would immediately stop drawing and turn his portrait face down on the bed so I couldn't see what he was sketching. When I first observed this mysterious behavior, I was like, *Fuck him and his drawings; I don't care about that shit.* But when I carried my thoughts back to it, I realized that we had been cellmates for over a year, and I had never seen any of his drawings. Nor to my knowledge had he ever sold any of his artwork throughout the prison compound for commissary. I thought to myself, *That's weird, ain't it?*

It's unnatural and ungodly to be caged in with another man. I thought I was trippin' again because these cells do have a way of playing tricks on your mind. So to test my theory, I drank sixty-four ounces of water hella fast; an hour later, I was pissing *hard* about every five minutes. Lo and behold, every time I left that bunk, so did his drawing leave his hands. Instead of climbing down, a few times I even jumped off the top bunk to see what the fuck he was drawing. But he was too fast for me. He would hold his precious drawing up against his chest like an old lady clutching her purse as she walks through a group of thugs. (By the way, what's the skin color of the group of thugs in your mind?) Moreover, X-Man would also slam his drawing face down, hard and fast like a young Shaquille O'Neal.

The curiosity was killing me. I had no choice but to let it go because whatever he was drawing wasn't any of my fucking business (rule one). I could rifle through his things whenever he would leave the cell, but no matter how much I wanted to see, I refused to do that because those are the actions of a bitch ass nigga, and I'm far from that, so I left it alone.

Several months had passed before I was given an opportunity to see the incarcerated Picasso's fine artwork. Menard was cracking down on the number of items an inmate could keep outside of his property box, so an "effective immediately" memorandum was given to every resident. Plainly put, this memo stated that whenever you left your cell everything had to be stored inside of your property box except the TV, radio, fan, lamp, one pair of shoes, toothbrush, toothpaste, soap, deodorant, and soiled laundry. Anything outside of those items would be confiscated and disciplinary action would be taken.

Confiscation is a nice way of announcing, "We're going to throw your shit in the garbage." Disciplinary action is a hardline way of declaring, "Then we're taking your ass to segregation." Don't get it twisted; the officers despised new memos just as much as we do. Why? A new memorandum meant they had extra work to do outside of counting inmates, running chow, and turning keys. Trust me, a majority of the correctional officers that I've encountered are lazier than a motherfucker. But rules are rules and they have to be enforced.

Officer Dickface worked on our gallery five days a week. Being impartial, Officer Dickface was cool in a sense because he never stood on every single rule, but he was still a bitch. Let's take the current memo for example. Say I left an extra pair of gym shoes and a Snickers bar outside of my property box when I went to chow. He wouldn't just throw my jumpers and food in the garbage before taking me to segregation. He'd toss everything that I own around the cell like a mini hurricane came through and leave my cellmate's possessions alone. That's what I mean by "he was cool in a sense" because nobody wants to lose a pair of gym shoes or food to the garbage can when money is so hard to come by in prison.

In the same breath, that's some bitch ass shit to do because he's throwing around drawings, letters, and pictures from our kids and obituaries of loved ones lost. What if it was the anniversary of my grandmother's death and I'm consumed with thoughts of her so I accidentally leave out an item or two, and Officer Dickface tosses my cell and in the process slings my grandmother's obituary on the cold, hard, dirty prison floor?

If I justifiably knocked his front teeth out, I would get hand-cuffed and then brutally beaten by his fellow employees and friends in retaliation. The whole incident would be written up like I'm the bad guy, a convict who had gone crazy and given in to the pressures of incarceration. Instead of the whole truth. Yeah, I may have overre-acted, but it was the officer's abuse of authority and unprofessional-ism that started this whole situation. There are rules and procedures for a reason, Officer Dickface.

One Monday morning, X-Man and I received call passes for the prison law library. The law library is the only place in the joint where inmates can go to for two hours a week to research their crim-inal and civil cases, file motions, and check out various other reading materials. If you don't have a court-ordered legal deadline to meet, two hours a week in the law library is all you got coming in Menard and that's fucked up.

FYI, 65 to 70 percent of the inmates in Menard Correctional Center will never see the streets again. How much of that percentage do you believe is actually innocent? How much of that percentage do you think is illiterate, mentally retarded, and mentally ill? How much of that percentage do you think received an overly excessive sentence because it was a "get tough on crime" election season? How much of that percentage do you think was used as a stepping-stone for an overzealous prosecutor to make a name for him or herself instead of prosecuting in the interest of justice? How much of that percentage do you think had an overworked and underpaid public defender as a defense attorney? And how much of that percentage do you believe are victims of "impoverishenza"? "Justice delayed is justice denied," says Dr. Martin Luther King Jr.

Now with all that said, do you honestly think that two hours a week is an adequate amount of time for an inmate to spend in the law library fighting for his life? No one should have to unjustly die in prison when it is clear that there were other tangible factors involved with boxing him in. I don't know how Menard is getting away with this shit. The law says in *Bounds v. Smith*, 430 U.S. 817, 97 S. CT. 1491 (1977), and I am paraphrasing: every inmate should receive no less than five hours a week in the law library to prepare for whatever. The warden of Menard Correctional Center is loudly saying with the way he's running his facility, "Fuck the law, I am the law." But when I act accordingly, I'm handcuffed and punished.

I just so happened to be walking in the front of the line while returning from the law library. When I reentered the building, one of my homies signaled to me that Officer Dickface had been in my cell.

Damn, what did I leave out? I thought to myself as I jogged up the staircase.

When I finally made it to the door, our cell had been tossed. X-Man's possessions were thrown everywhere, and my property was exactly where I had left it.

What the fuck is this? I screamed in my head when I finally saw what this sick motherfucker had been drawing for the past year and a half. Guess what this nigga was drawing? Go ahead, guess.

Naw, you all wrong; it was a picture of a man with a big-ass were-wolf head. This werewolf head was similar to the jackals in Egyptian pyramid hieroglyphics. The facial expression of this werewolf's head was angry and growling; his eyes bulged out and his lion-sized teeth dripped with saliva. This monstrosity had the body of a man who looked strong as hell and was ripped to death. He was all beefed up like a Black Bruce Lee. This thing had gargoyle feet and hands with razor-sharp talons for nails. Those extremities are unmistakably used for climbing trees and scaling tall buildings.

The werewolf/man/gargoyle was wearing a pair of tattered blue jean shorts and he was peering to the left at an innocent-looking White woman with long dark hair. This super predator appeared to be stalking her and was moments from attack. Now check this out, the little White lady was completely naked with some big-ass porn star titties and nipples the size of number three pencil erasers, and she was squatting over a dirty bucket, pissing. I couldn't make this shit up. She was pissing! And this evil-ass nigga drew the exact same drawing over and over again at least three hundred times, and they were thrown all over the cell floor. Can you picture that?

Some things in life you should never see, and this is one of them 'cause I can't get that shit out of my head. I took a thousand unwanted mental pictures in less than a nanosecond and kept it moving as I walked down to cell 724 and greeted my Muslim brother Aziz.

"As-salam alaykum."

"Walaykum as-salam. What's wrong with you?" he said, reading my distraught demeanor.

"I'll holler at you later," I responded and continued, "What you on down here?"

"Just watching an old Cubs game. You know, if I did more of this in the world instead of running them streets I probably wouldn't be here now. Blah blah blah..." And on he went, because after the word *now*, I didn't hear a thing he said. I was too busy trying to understand what the fuck I just saw.

"Gilford, come lock up!" Officer Dickface yelled, snapping me out of my confusion.

I looked his way and saw X-Man stepping into our cell. For several minutes, he and the gallery officer argued back and forth. No doubt X-Man was checking him about the mistreatment of his satanic artwork. After they had words, Dickface screamed again, "Gilford, lock up! This is your second direct order!"

"All right man, hold fast!" I abruptly hollered.

"Lil brother, lock up before you get in trouble," Aziz chimed in.

"Be cool akhi. It's a lot going on that you don't know about," I snapped back.

"Mr. Gilford, this is your third and final direct order—*lock the fuck up!*"

All I could think of doing was giving X-Man enough time to pick that perverted shit up off the floor and act like I ain't seen a thing. I figured I'd be safe as always if he believed that I never laid eyes upon his depraved drawings. So I walked as slow as I possibly could to cell 720, stepped in, and *boom!*—the door was slammed shut behind me.

"Our cell got tossed. I left about nine tapes out so that bitch-ass officer threw my drawings everywhere."

"Oh yeah," I said as I looked around the cell floor like I was ready to aid him in retrieving his pictures. "I don't see nothing cuzo."

"Yeah, I picked everything up before you came in," X-Man responded.

I kicked my shoes off, jumped in the bunk, lay back, and prayed, *LORD, how you gonna help me out of this one?*

What would you do if you were me?

CHAPTER 3

The Crazy Boy

I landed at Danville Correctional Center in the winter of 2012. I placed all my property into a rolling cart and headed toward house 3, B wing, upper tier, cell 71. When I made it to unit three, Officer Friendly slid me a key on top of a piece of paper, and with his index finger pointing to a specific section. "Sign here."

"What's that for, you trying to set me up?" I responded, refusing to take the key.

Officer Friendly laughed and said, "No, I am not trying to set you up sir. Every inmate receives a key to his cell."

"I ain't going!"

He laughed again and tossed the key in my direction, forcing me to catch it midair. "Now sign here please."

I hesitantly signed the paper as Officer Friendly orally regurgitated what was written above the X mark for my signature. "If you lose the key, it'll cost you twenty dollars to replace it. *Next!*"

As I stepped on B wing, there wasn't any anger, malice, rage, or violence floating in the atmosphere. Not feeling the negative tension that I normally felt upon entering a new facility really scared the shit out of me. So much so that my fight-flight-or-freeze mechanism got stuck on red alert and I couldn't turn it off. My demeanor must have unmasked the anxiety, because every person I passed looked at me like I was crazier than two motherfuckers. And those suspicious stares only sent my fear levels into the stratosphere. It's amazing what you'll adapt to in prison and accept as normal when it is actually the apex of abnormality. I silently prayed.

Oh GOD, please protect me 'cause I don't know what's about to happen.

Allah heard my prayer. I was blessed to be housed with this smooth young brother from Decatur named Fat Man (but he wasn't fat at all; go figure). As I lay in the top bunk, he walked back and forth in our little abode, sharing the particulars of this medium-security prison. He moved with such style and grace and spoke from a position of power like the commercialized Billy D. Williams who had just finished off a tall can of Colt 45. I ain't gonna stunt; he was cooler than two anorexic lovers in an air-conditioned room with the ceiling fan on, and I admired his swag.

Every single time that I've been caged in with a new cellmate, it takes about two or three weeks to pass before I get to see the "real" him. Eighteen years into a thirty-two-and-a-half-year bid, I finally ran into the exception to that rule. The way Fat Man introduced himself was the way he continued to be. And six months easily breezed by before he laid the *kaboom!*

"Sheed, I'm finta move in the cell with one of my homies from D-Town."

"Come on man," I joylessly responded.

"Me and him ran the streets together, and I wanna hang out with him before he go to the crib."

How could I argue with that? So I feebly took a swing at their brotherhood.

"Man, you gonna go down there, get in trouble, and jag your outdate."

"You know I ain't on that, and if he is, that's on him, 'cause ain't no nigga finta stop me from getting to my baby boy!" he said with emphasis.

I felt he truly meant that last statement because in the one hundred and eighty-three days that we peacefully lived together, that was the first time that he had ever raised his voice.

Seven days later, Fat Man moved out, and like clockwork Mr. JD dragged right on in. JD was short, pudgy, with a big-ass head like a retarded rottweiler. And this nigga had the nerve to have a li'l Kobe Bryant afro on the top of that worn-out medicine ball. Where do these niggas come from?

"What's up man, my name's Rasheed," I said as I helped him slide his property boxes into the cell.

"They call me JD," he responded with a smile.

I was about to relax, but for some reason his smile looked fake, like he was forcing it upon his face. Right there was an immediate red flag because he was being weird for no reason at all.

Beeeep! Offsides, on the defense; ten-yard penalty; repeat first down.

But at the same time I had to pick up the flag because what if he was just as afraid of living in a cell with me as I was of being trapped in a cage with him?

Beeep! Bad call; the initial ruling on the field stands; still first down.

Anyway, he had all his electronics and a box full of food, and he was from the southside of Chicago. Check, check, and more positive checks. He was a taxi driver by trade and could hold a conversation and think a little bit. JD caught me up on all the latest hood shit and even shared a few of those sexually comedic taxi-driving tall tales. I began to relax, thinking, *I done came up again.*

Oh, how I was so fracking wrong. The very first day, later that evening, during the middle of one of our many conversations, he turned his back to me, took a piss in the toilet, wiped the metal seat with a rolled-up wad of tissue paper, and flushed. But he didn't wash his fucking hands, and he continued to talk like he didn't just touch his man meat.

Relax, I wasn't watching him while he was pissing; I caught all of that with my peripheral vision. I'm in a seven-by-ten-foot two-man cell, so his derriere was literally three feet away from my face. Honestly, at that distance, if he were to fart, I would smell his ass before he would, and maybe even taste it a little.

Kids, stay out of prison if you don't like the taste and smell of another man's ass. And if you do, sign up, and you will never be disappointed at the variety of shit smells that the prison industrial complex has in store for you.

Please let this be a mistake, I thought to myself before I went into verbal judo mode.

"Hey, JD, I'm not trying to be nosy or disrespectful, but I noticed you took a piss and you didn't wash your hands."

"Yeah you saw right," he standoffishly responded.

"Why wouldn't you wash your hands when you just touched your *swiller*?"

"I don't touch my dick when I piss."

"What?"

I sort of chuckled, not because what he voiced was funny; I laughed because I couldn't believe what he just said to me. This nigga talking like he got an autonomous firehose dick. How do you respond to something like that? "I don't touch my dick when I piss."

I decided to move pass the dick touching and attack from the pissy tissue angle.

"What about when you wipe urine off the toilet seat with the tissue paper? Don't you think you need to wash your hands then?"

"Naw, 'cause I don't get no piss on the seat," he replied with a smirk.

Is this nigga serious or is he fucking with me? Becoming annoyed, I retorted, "So why wipe the toilet seat at all if you piss like a god?"

"That's for the backlash of toilet water that pops out from the force of my piss," he stated matter-of-factly.

"Well, why don't you clean the toilet water from your hands then?"

"I use enough tissue when I wipe, so the toilet water never touch my fingers."

He had me right there, and it made sense, especially in crazy language. I initially thought I had a Chi-Town Fat Man in the cell with me. But he turned out to be another nasty motherfucker. So I fell all the way back after that fruitful toiletry discussion.

Danville Correctional Center is a laid-back medium-security prison. I'm not advocating police-ism in any sense, but in the interest of truth, it's safe to say that the abundance of good coppers in DCC far outweigh the totality of cranks.

Medium-security prison means extra-extra privileges and even more time outside of your cell to move around and sniff some fresh air. In addition to yard and gym time, every day, we get two separate dayroom periods, one in the AM and the other in the PM, lasting about an hour and a half respectively.

The dayroom is a twenty-five-by-hundred-twenty-five-foot space that has six strategically placed old-school phone booths on the front end. These booths are made of thinly meshed metal minus the front door and Plexiglas that Clark Kent would need to change into Superman. Furthermore, upfront on the upper and lower tier, in plain view of the observation pod, is a shower section with two individual shower heads. A plastic shower curtain hangs about four feet in the air and ends about two feet from the ground. There is just enough plastic to cover your sex organs from the viewing observation officer. But, most importantly, the height and length of the plastic hinders homosexual behavior and equally keeps an inmate from being raped or sexually abused.

On the backend of the wing are four spaciously placed tables, with four connecting backless McDonald seats, all of which are bolted to the floor. If you haven't figured it out by now, this in-house recreational area is spacious enough for fifty men to use the phone, take showers, socialize, and play card games, chess, dominoes, Scrabble, or whatever.

What I love the most about dayroom time is the mere fact that I can take a shit now, in the cell, without the company of my roommate, 'cause he can pop out and go about his business. Then I can sit butt-naked on the commode with one dirty sock on and do the damn thang. It's the little things baby, the little things.

Three weeks passed with Mr. Pissy Hands. In order to stay healthy, rest my worrying mind, and keep the peace, I would soap up the sink, light switch, and any other communal area before usage. Yeah, I went through a lot of soap but at least I got to shower twice a day if I wanted as opposed to showering only twice a week like in

Menard maximum-security prison. Fuck this nasty-ass creep; I ain't trying to go backward.

One day, we got served some half-cooked chicken for lunch. My mind told me not to eat the shit. But my appetite got the better of me. Take note, I said it here first, the chicken stereotype is true: "all Black folks love chicken." Me even more so because I ate it at the risk of salmonella poisoning. In defense of my people, there ain't nothing strange surrounding the reasons why *we* love chicken so. On top of it being a delicious treat, we fancy yard bird because we grew up eating it. And why are we orientated toward poultry? Chicken is one of the least expensive foods on the market. Any right-minded person will tell you that a nice percentage of African Americans are in bad shape financially. So when you're poor, the more bang that you can get out of your buck is always a plus; hence the climb in poultry sales. Now, why are *we* as a people in such poor financial health? You can blame slavery, institutional racism, marginalization, or the White, capitalistic, patriarchal society (America). Pick one.

Equally, White people love fried chicken just as much as Black people. When I worked in Downtown Chicago, I used to see White folks in those dual restaurants and food courts waiting for some Kentucky Fried Chicken. The KFC lines were always around the corner and out the door. A brother couldn't get any chicken downtown with only an hour-long lunch break.

"Welcome to McDonald's! May I take your order please?"

"Ummm... Yeah...let me get a Big Mac and a ..."

You White motherfuckers love some chicken too. And rightly so; it's inexpensive and delicious.

Well, anyway, that half-cooked chicken gave me the bubble guts for real. So I was forced to shit on three different occasions with JD in the cell. It's weird defecating in a pantry-sized room with another man. Even though we're "allowed" to hang a sheet for privacy, it still feels like I'm taking a dump in a grammar school restroom with a missing stall door. And my cellmate is sitting on the bathroom sink across from me, watching me shit. Yeah, that's one way to describe it. After the third Black Hawk Down, I soaped my hands, and lay down in the fetal position because my stomach was still killing me.

"Rasheed you good?" JD said.

"Naw man, that chicken fucked me up. The judicial system ain't shit."

JD laughed, and I followed suit because the system ain't force me to eat that paleolithic chicken.

"They got me too," JD said as he jumped off the top bunk and hung his sheet to defecate. About fifteen minutes passed before JD's exorcism was complete. He got up, removed the sheet, and jumped straight into his bed without washing his motherfucking hands. *Oh hell no!* Fuck verbal judo; I went straight into attack mode.

"JD, why you ain't wash your hands and you just got through taking a shit?"

"'Cause my fingers don't touch my asshole, the tissue do."

"What?"

"I'm thirty-two years old. I know how to wipe my ass without getting shit on my fingers!"

"What about when you stick your hand in the toilet to wipe? Don't you think the impurities on the inside and the splashing toilet water needs to be washed off?"

"Naw, I'm good on that too, 'cause I lift my ass high enough to where my hand never lands inside the toilet."

Now I was going crazy because the shit he was saying was starting to make sense to me. Then I heard my mom's voice inside my head like the Jedi master Obi-Wan Kenobi would pop up in Luke Skywalker's mind whenever he was doubting himself.

You ain't crazy; that nasty motherfucker CRAZY!

So I fought on.

"Why you scared to clean your hands?"

"I ain't scared. That's just a waste of soap."

"Here!" I said, attempting to pass him a fresh bar of Irish Spring.

"Naw, you can keep that. If I ain't gonna waste mine, why would I waste yours?"

I had to take a seat and collect my thoughts before I DDT'd this motherfucker.

Anger is not working, and I definitely can't beat this nigga ass because he gone have shit residue everywhere. Then they gonna ship

37

me out this sweet-ass joint faster than Usain Bolt running after an Olympic gold medal. I got a key to my cell… I got a key to my cell… I got a key to my cell… So what can I do? Hopefully my sense of humor can get me out of this one.

I stood up, looked him straight in his eyes, and said, "JD, I been locked up for over eighteen years straight and I have never indulged in any homosexual activities. Whether you get shit on your fingers or not, if you don't wash your hands after you defecate then touch the water buttons or the light switch, in my mind you're smearing dookie everywhere. Then if I come behind you and press the same buttons or hit the light, I feel like my hand is touching the bittersweet softness of your asshole. I been locked up a long time and I can only resist for so long. Please don't make a fag out of me," I said, ending with my hands together in the prayer position.

He fell out laughing, and I kept going.

"I'm a need you to wash your hands after you piss too, 'cause if you don't and I touch what you touch, I feel like I'm jagging your dick." He laughed even louder, and I kept chopping away at his insanity with my jokes.

"What do you call a hand that's on your swiller that you don't know?"

"*A hand job!*" he barked out loud in the midst of his laughter.

"Naw, that's called a sneaky motherfucker. Nigga, I don't want to know you intimately and I definitely don't wanna be a sneaky motherfucker, so wash your *hands*!"

I laughed along with him because I finally got through to this crazy motherfucker. Some people may say that JD is just trifling but not crazy, and I get that. In defense of my position, you got to be crazy if you think you can take a shit and not wash your hands, smearing fecal matter everywhere. Even the teachers of Socrates, the Pre-Socrates, from the ancient city of Kemet or Kush say, and I'm paraphrasing, "If you don't wash your hands after releasing body waste, then you are a crazy motherfucker." And I tend to agree.

Real talk: with us being creatures of habit, I believe he only washed his hands when I was in his presence. I bet you whenever I left the cell, he would take a forty-ounce malt liquor piss or a "Macho

Man" Randy Savage shit and purposely abstain from washing his hands to spite me. Then he'd touch my TV buttons, fan, tape player, and pillowcase just because he could. *Prison sucks!*

What would you do if you were me?

CHAPTER 4

The Straight Creep

When you're on the precarious road of life, whether you're in the free world or in prison, you pick up real friends along the way and discard the rest.

One of my home boyz told me, "Sheed, you got to be careful in them li'l camps 'cause the lower level you go, the more creeped out them niggas be."

I laughed, but in time I learned that there wasn't anything funny to be taken from his forewarning.

In Danville, during the second week in Ramadan around the end of September 2015, I received a new cellmate. He was a special delivery from Lawrenceville Correctional Center. My prior roomie got a job with the dietary department so he happily moved to the workers' deck. All the things that I had encountered during my extensive incarceration could never have prepared me for this moment. A five-foot-eleven, midforties Black man with an angry demeanor, a beer belly, and short-ass arms stood in the doorway.

"How you doing brah? My name's Rasheed," I said, sticking out my fist.

"Yeah, I'm K-Dub," he aggressively retorted, refusing to give me some dap.

I didn't take his response personally. He could have been having a bad day. Plus I was in the thick of Ramadan, so my emotions could have been at an all-time high. Ramadan is the ninth month of the Islamic calendar. Around this time of the year, Muslims all over the world abstain from food and drink from sunrise till sunset. In addition, we also refrain from lying, cursing, backbiting, lusting, or anything else displeasing to Allah. Twenty-nine to thirty days of this kind of abstinence has you "open" mentally, spiritually, physically, emotionally, sexually, and intellectually in ways you could never imagine. This "openness" is hard to explain, so I'm a just leave it there and say, fast during the month of Ramadan a day or two, maybe more, and you'll see firsthand what I'm talking about.

"You want me to help you with your stuff?"

"No."

So I slid on the bunk and kept reading my Holy Quran. Several hours of uncomfortable silence passed before we spoke again.

"Rasheed, can I get these three pegs over here? 'Cause I don't want my stuff all by the door."

"Yeah, just switch 'em around."

"Naw, I don't want to touch your shit. I'll just wait till you move it."

"Man gone move that stuff."

"I can wait until you get a chance to move it."

Drilled into the wall in every cell, next to the door about eye level, is a wooden coatrack with six reasonably spaced four-inch timber pegs extending out to hang clothing. His willingness to wait on me was a total farce because he stood in the middle of the floor, staring at the coatrack. And the tone he used was prison lingo for, "Nigga, hurry up and move your shit so I can get situated."

So I jumped on up and shifted my clothing to the far end of the rack.

What did you get out of that little conversation that K-Dub and I just had? Go ahead, take a moment, and think about it. Read it again if you have to, because there is a lot being said about his character with that little back-and-forth.

K-Dub just told me in so many words that he's paranoid and extremely territorial. Moreover, he clearly stated in no uncertain terms that while we're living together, he ain't gonna touch my shit and I better not touch his shit. Understand? The more we converse, the more I'll be able to figure him out and move accordingly so we can coexist within this little space.

I've had plenty of angry and territorial cellmates. The initial formula for survival is the same minus a few underlying personality adjustments here and there:

1. I'll never engage or start a conversation with him. Angry people say angry shit, and I'm hanging onto my happiness by a thread. I don't need his words pulling at that string.
2. I'll never touch his property unless given permission, which is extremely hard to do when you have two grown men crammed into a custom-made panic room for a malnourished midget.
3. I will never take his angry demeanor or territoriality personal. He got a right to be mad; he was judicially kidnapped from his loved ones and snatched away from all the sweet old liberties of American life. You'd be pissed too.

Moreover, his territorial issues could have stemmed from cellmates who'd come before me. Any one of them could have broken an electronic of his or stolen some of his property. So if he wants to put police tape around his penitentiary possessions for protection, so be it; I understand.

The few times that he spoke to me after the coatrack incident were all negative, laden with expletives, and he often highlighted the fact that he had fifteen more years of incarceration to complete before being released. His energy-draining rants were a slick way of saying, "I'm a mad, bad motherfucker and I ain't got shit to lose."

I heard him loud and clear. Normally, to put someone like this in their place, I would fight fire with fire and share my penitentiary pedigree with something like, "Nigga, that ain't shit. I done over fifteen years, and a large percentage of that time was spent in *the Pit*."

The Pit is what we call Menard's Maximum-Security Prison for short. Why? Someone took a heap of dynamite and blew a ninety-foot hole into the ground the size of a small town and built a penal institution inside that space. Then they filled the joint with three thousands of Illinois's convicted and extremely dangerous gang chiefs, murderers, rapists, drug dealers, and all-around low-life bastards, like the pit of hell/hades spoken of so freely in the Holy Bible for unrepentant sinners.

For the first time in a long time, I chose not to share my incarcerated background. I was too busy enjoying the blessed month of Ramadan to engage in any psychological cell games. My unwillingness to utilize a successful negative formula, to combat his negativity, and turn this whole situation semipositive would come back later on and bite me in the ass.

My penitentiary super-jerk meter is top shelf. So whenever I come into contact with a hateful motherfucker, I can just feel the loathing radiating off his presence. The tension in the cell with this crank reeked of such vileness for three days straight, but it felt more like three weeks.

Day four, dinner tray in hand, I came back to the cell cute as a button after indulging in engageful conversations and Congregational salat. I hadn't eaten in about fifteen hours. So you know I was more than ready to wolf down a double burger with fries and fat-boyishly enjoy a big chunk of white cake with chocolate icing heavily smeared on top. Black on white baby!

One of the many joys of Ramadan is the breaking of the fast. I've never known food to smell or taste so good. After fasting, you could be eating a plain saltine cracker and get to smacking your lips like, "Is this paprika I taste?"

Anyway, I opened the cell door and was immediately smacked in the face with the smell of diesel fuel, like I just strolled into an overbooked diesel-automotive mechanic's shop. *What the fuck is that!* sounds off in my mind. Instantly, my head began to hurt as I looked for the cause of such foulness. I found nothing, so I'm forced to violate one of my rules of survival with an angry nigga.

"K-Dub, what's that smell?"

"What smell?"

"Come on man!"

"Oh, that's my fan."

"Why it's blowing out that smell?"

"It needed some oil. I ain't have none so I used hair grease!" he angrily retorted as if he was done with my line of questioning.

At that point I didn't care how he felt 'cause he done fucked up my whole meal and he got my head hurting.

"Why would you use hair grease? Better yet, why do you think your fan needs any oil at all? Did you read the instructions when you bought it?"

His silence revealed his stupidity and lack of concern for my questions.

"You got the whole cell stanking. You plan on cleaning your fan anytime soon?"

K-Dub exhaled loud and hard like I'm the problem, then said, "It ain't bothering me!"

I think to myself, ain't that a bitch; I know that smell is fucking with him, but he know it's affecting me more because I'm fasting. And just when I was about to go HAM, my taqwa steps in. *Rasheed, it's Ramadan. Be the bigger man and wash the fan.*

"You mind if I wash it then? 'Cause that smell got my head hurting."

"If you break my fan, you gone buy me a new one!" he declared threateningly.

I almost said, "Nigga, I'm a break your ass in here if you keep talking tuff!" But it was Ramadan, Ramadan, Ramadan, so I humbled myself further.

"If I break it while cleaning, I'll pay for a new one."

"Go head then nigga," he Scarface'ly retorted.

I laughed and shook my head because I was starting to think that this creep's taking my meekness for weakness. Meekness is never weakness; it's strength under control, and I'm as strong as they come.

When I finished cleaning his fan, I plugged it up and turned it on, and K-Dub smiled like an evil villain then sarcastically said, "You did a good job. It's blowing better than the first day I bought it."

My primary thought at his taunting was, did he do this on purpose, knowing I was fasting so I would have to clean his fan or feel sick? Affirmative, because his grease-laden fan was full of dust.

Like the tortoise that raced the hare, six more days crawled by before we spoke again. It was lunchtime, and I popped out to holler at Big Trav before he left for chow. In the middle of our conversation, K-Dub rudely interrupted.

"Rasheed dump the garbage!"

Quick side note: In prison, there's penitentiary etiquette about everything. For example, if two people are talking and you need to holler at one of them, you must say "excuse me" before you interrupt their conversation. You can't just bust in and start talking like what you have to say is more important than their discussion. Actions like that are considered disrespectful and a quick way to get your ass kicked.

Me and Big Trav glanced K-Dub's way and went right back to talking like he never existed. While kicking the boe-boes, I happened to notice with my peripheral vision that K-Dub had gone in and out of the cell two more times before the line left out for chow.

Every cell has a small one-by-one-by-one-foot plastic rectangular garbage receptacle. When I came into the cell and looked into the trash can, it was less than halfway full. I thought out loud, "This nigga trippin'. Ain't no garbage even in there. And why he ain't dump it himself?"

I went back to my favorite episode of *Seinfeld*, the one where they all bet money to see who could go the longest without masturbating, and I laughed until the lunch line returned.

"Rasheed, why you ain't dump that garbage?"

"What's wrong with your hands?" I responded, and K-Dub snatched up the trash can and dumped it into a larger wastebasket outside the cell.

"I don't like a full garbage can 'cause that's gone bring bugs!" K-Dub announced as he slammed the empty can to the floor.

"Man, it wasn't hardly no garbage in there!" I expressed with a mug on my face.

"It's still gone bring bugs!"

"Look here man, you walked in and out this cell on two different occasions after you rudely interrupted my conversation. Why

45

you ain't dump the garbage then, since you're so concerned about bugs?"

"Ummm… Ahhh…I—"

"Hold on, Saturday when I soaped up the walls and cleaned the floor, I didn't ask you to help me. Did I?" Not waiting for an answer, I continued, "So why you need me to help you dump some garbage?"

He just found out that I was intense with common sense.

"I'm just trying to keep bugs out our cell," he rightly stated.

"Where is all these bugs you keep talking about anyway? Man you trippin', don't involve me in that!"

Right then I realized I was angry. I quickly turned down so I wouldn't knowingly violate my fast. About thirty minutes passed, and K-Dub jumped out of the bunk and did something that caught me totally off guard.

"Rasheed, I apologize about the garbage. You right. I was trippin', 'cause you ain't ask me to clean up nothing around here."

"It's cool man, ain't no big thang."

His apology felt sincere as he looked me in the eyes for the very first time. Honestly, I thought we'd be all right after that incident.

Four more days passed before our next confrontation. I popped out the cell to empty a "full" wastebasket like any normal-minded person would do. I left the cell door open because the communal trash can is literally five pistol-dueling paces away. When I returned moments later, I was greeted by that old familiar K-Dub scowl.

"Rasheed, why you keep leaving that door open?"

"What's wrong now?"

"You keep leaving the door open! What if somebody ran up in here on me while I was getting dressed?"

"Run in on you? Man ain't nobody finta run in on you. You in Danville, not Statesville!"

"That don't mean shit. I'm still in prison!"

Feeling my anger boil during the blessed month of Ramadan, I chose to go into a 402 Conference.

"So what you want me to do? Lock the door whenever I leave the cell even if I'm taking a few steps to the garbage?"

"Yeah!"

"All right, it won't happen again." Alhamdulillah, I bowed out gracefully.

This nigga acting like he some supreme hood serial killer that everybody's trying to murder to earn their stripes. I bet you this mark was a scary-ass crackhead or a sneaky-ass dope fiend in the world, and after being drug-free for a while because of incarceration, all of a sudden he's a lean, mean killing machine. Lucky number thirteen is what I said in my head as I counted the number of days that I've been housed with this crank. Lucky number thirteen.

The sun rose and set two more times, drama free, before we bumped heads again. It was afternoon dayroom time. I patiently waited for K-Dub to pop out, then I began making the proper preparations to take a nice dump. First, I slid a piece of paper in the door. This piece of paper is the universal penitentiary sign that says to all those around, "I'm Busy, Do Not Disturb!"

Next, I lined the cold, hard, metal seat with toilet tissue, got butt-ass naked, put on my lucky sock, and jumped on the motorcycle. I was smack-dab in the middle of shitting like a dog when I hear K-Dub screaming my name at the top of his lungs from the dayroom.

"Rasheed! *Rasheed!* RASHEED! You through yet?"

I thought out loud, "Is this nigga crazy? I know he sees the sign in the door; why he hollering my name like that?"

I looked at my timepiece; ain't nothing but five minutes that went by. Fuck him, he can holler until his throat box bursts for all I care. And holler he did, over and over again.

"Rasheed! What's taking so long?"

About five more minutes passed before I was done. As I calmly reached back to wipe my ass, I saw this nigga face in the chuckhole staring at me.

A chuckhole is like an institutional peephole that can be utilized from both sides of the door. It's a two-by-four-foot, eye-level, semi-grated metal square that's used by the correctional officers to count and observe an inmate's behavior.

When our eyes locked, he mugged up and walked away like I done fucked up his day. I screamed in my head, *Is this nigga a fag? I'm checking this creep as soon as I get through.*

I wiped my ass, washed my hands, got dressed, removed the sign, and pushed the door all the way open. The month of Ramadan had ended the day before, so I was more than ready to beat his ass for today's stunt and for his attitude in times gone by.

He came in and slammed the door behind him. *Boom!* His back was all hunched up, like a silverback gorilla with some little-ass arms. I wasn't impressed or scared in the least.

"Man why you hollering my name like you crazy while I'm on the shitter?"

"My bag, I thought you had the sign in the door for no reason."

"Naw, fuck 'my bag,' why you hollering my name like you crazy?"

With that being the first time he had ever heard me drop an F bomb, his eyes got big, his posture straightened up, and his demeanor and tone softened.

"I done had cellies that keep the sign in the door for hours, and when I looked in, they ain't doing nothing but watching TV."

"Hours! Nigga the sign was in the door about five minutes before you started acting crazy!"

He just stood there looking stupid.

Real talk: I wanted to steal on his ass. But the Holy Month had just ended, and the same humility I displayed during Ramadan should be held throughout the entire year. So I turned down and decided to use my charisma to open his eyes.

"K-Dub, have I ever done anything in this cell that would lead you to believe that I would purposely keep the sign in the door?"

"No."

"So why did you think I'd be on something like that?"

"You might've forgot it."

"You didn't give me a chance to forget. It was only in there like five minutes!"

He was still trying to justify this creep shit. It was clear that my charisma wasn't working. Inspired by my favorite *Seinfeld* episode, I warped into comedy mode.

"Look at it like this brah. What if I was in here masturbating and about to bust the best nut ever, then you get to calling my name? I know you don't want me thinking about you at the *point of no return*," I said, emphasizing the last four words.

He smiled, started laughing, then said, "All right Rasheed, you win. As long as that sign is in the door, you ain't gonna hear nothing from me."

"That's all I ask."

"Can I ask you one more question?"

"Shoot."

"Why was you naked on the toilet with one sock on?"

"Why was you looking at me? You wasn't even supposed to see that!"

And we laughed some more.

Two dog days later, I was knocked out asleep on the left side of my body, facing the wall with a sheet pulled completely over my head. I was slightly awakened by the sensation of something tugging at my sheet down by my boxer shorts. I lay still, fully awake, not sure if I was dreaming or if something had actually touched me. A few moments later, I felt someone pulling at my boxer shorts again. I quickly removed the sheet from over my head and sat up. I saw K-Dub arm move to the top bunk as if he was reaching for something upon his bed. Although I was within my full right to go berserk without question, all I wanted to know was, why? No anger, no malice, only *why?*

"Man, why was you tugging on my sheet down by my boxer shorts?"

"Oh, my bag, my knee must've hit you when I was reaching for my ID."

"Man I know the difference between a push and a pull. Why was you touching me while I was sleep?"

"Motherfucker I told you that was my knee! Wasn't nobody touching you!" he said, screaming loud as ever.

"I don't know what you getting loud fo, I'm just trying to get some clarity about this situation."

"Fuck clarity, you accusing me of something I ain't do!"

"All right man, I'm gone from the situation. *Please* stop talking to me."

K-Dub never lowered his tone and he kept cussing and fussing like he was checking me. I looked at my watch; it was 4:16 a.m. I put my gym shorts on, stepped into my shower shoes, and washed my face. K-Dub was fully dressed because he had an early morning call pass to the health care unit. The more I thought about what just took place, the more my blood boiled, and the loudness of his voice faded into the background.

Was this nigga just feeling on me like I was a bitch or something?

Then flashbacks of all our run-ins rapidly shot through my mind like a sexual assault victim on a Lifetime Channel movie special: the coatrack and garbage can incident, me washing his fan, his predatory eyes upon my ass while I was defecating, and now him touching on me.

The cell door popped open as I put my face towel away. K-Dub walked out and slammed the room door hard as hell. *Boom!*

That was it; I couldn't hold back any longer. Fuck waiting until 7:00 a.m. shift change to holler at a lieutenant to get moved, fuck this sweet-ass joint, fuck everything. It's time for me to speak in a language that I know he would understand: VIOLENCE!

So I moved swiftly to the chuckhole and hollered out, "What that supposed to mean?"

K-Dub yelled back, "Pop the door and I'll show you!"

I pushed the cell door button, but it did not open. Right then and there, time slowed down even though it was moving hella fast. I looked down and realized that I didn't have my gym shoes on as K-Dub slid his key into the keyhole.

Fuck! No time to slide 'em on now. I gotta go barefoot, I thought in my head as I kicked my shower shoes off and to the side.

When K-Dub turned his key, the door popped, and he snatched it open with his left hand and cocked his right hand back in an attempt to punch me in my eye.

K-Dub had an evil-ass look on his face similar to Freddy Kruger from *The Nightmare on Elm Street* when his razor-sharp knifed glove is up in the air and he's about to swing down upon a cornered teenage victim.

Quick side note: I wrestled for Chicago Vocational High School and I went Down State my junior year. Also, over the years of my incarceration, I've learned how to properly defend myself. Yes, I am a practitioner of "The Sweet Science." Then when you sprinkle on top of that my hood/penitentiary rage, I'm kind of like Liam Neeson from the movie *Taken*—I have a particular set of skills. No bullshit! Smile.

Anyway, his right hand was cocked back, and I went straight up the middle with an uppercut. *Bam!* His evil-ass demeanor was quickly replaced by one of surprise, and his knifed-glove/right hand disappeared from sight. After that, everything else was textbook. Like Coach Howell always said, "Throw punches with a purpose." And that I did.

I went straight to his head; jab, right hand, left uppercut, right hook, hook, and hook. I landed about eleven blows of an eighteen-punch combination, and this nigga hadn't dropped yet. He recovered and caught me with a one-two but wasn't much on it. The first one landed over my right eye, and I semislipped the second one because it only grazed the top of my head. I stepped back on an angle, and K-Dub smiled as if to say, *Yeah nigga, I'm still here!*

I doubled up the jab, and when he backed into a dayroom table, I threw the right hand. It landed on his chest. From there, I grabbed his neck and used my other hand to grab his outer right thigh and slammed him to the floor. *Boom!* Single-leg takedown. Coach Hall, my wrestling coach, would have been proud.

When we hit the floor, my hood/penitentiary rage took over and I slammed about four Donkey Kong hammer fists upon his face, before K-Dub finally broke and started screaming for mercy.

"All right Rasheed, that's enough!"

"I'm a man. Fuck you touching me for while I'm sleep? *You creep!*" I yelled as a correctional officer football-tackled me off him.

After being blindsided, I turned straight off as if a fighting bell had ended the round.

"Hey, officer. Can I get dressed?"

"Sure," he responded with a strange look on his face as we both rose from the ground.

I can only assume that he was trying to figure out how I went from Spartacus to Mr. Rogers all within a blink of an eye. I wanted to tell him that's just one difference between being trained and untrained; you tense when you throw and relax when you ain't.

I was cuffed up, taken to the health care unit, then segregation.

The only good thing about this whole situation of being housed with a straight creep is that as long as I'm in Danville Correctional Center, I'll never have to fight again. Why? My reputation will precede me. Between me and you, I don't like being violent. I'm only brave when I have to be, but with some niggas in prison, all they seem to understand is brutality.

What would you do if you were me?

CHAPTER 5

The Jealous Psycho

I used to be somewhat of a people pleaser. If an individual did not like me, I would go out of my way to prove to him or her that I was a good dude who deserves to be liked. In the summer of 2002, at the tender age of twenty-six, I was finally cured of an unyielding desire to seek acceptance from all the wrong people. Nowhere else but in "The Pit" could I have learned such a life-changing lesson.

"Gilford, you are going to seven gallery, cell twenty!" the East House front desk officer bellowed after viewing my ID card.

I moved my belongings up three flights of stairs in two trips. The physical process of the haul took less than ten minutes. My property box was hella empty after a series of segregation visits. I pushed all my things down to cell 20 like an Alaskan dog on the opposite end of a sled. Officer Dickface keyed me in about fifteen minutes later, smirked, and said, "Good luck." Then he slammed the door behind me.

"What's up cuzo? My name's Rasheed."

"I'm J-Rock."

"That's what's up," I responded as I struggled to read my new roomie.

While sizing him up, no immediate alarms went off, nor did I feel any negative tension. So I relaxed a little and busted open my last box of Nutty Bars. I had been dreaming about eating such heavenly treats for the last ten days of my stint in segregation. I attempted to pass J-Rock a couple of Nutty Bars, but he stopped me midway.

"Naw, I'm good."

"You sho?" I replied when he refused to accept my peace offering.

"Ahhh, yeah, just give me one tho," he said with a smile.

So we both chowed down while I sat back and basked in the glory of life outside the hole. It's always the little things baby, the little things.

J-Rock was a fair-looking, light-skinned, corpulent dude who stood about five foot ten. He appeared to be around my age, but he had teeth like the Walking Dead, which announced something different.

"Damn Rasheed, you eating another one?"

"Hell yeah, I been dreaming about these bad boys," I gleefully responded.

"How long was you in seg for?"

"Two months."

"For what?"

"I caught a sneak thief in my box, so I scraped him."

"Get the fuck outta here. Where your old cellie at now?"

"It wasn't my cellie. It was some other nigga on the gallery, so I dressed him on the walk."

"Oh! That was you who whupped dude in front of the West House and got to screaming, *'Don't Shoot! Don't shoot!'* at the catwalk officer when he cocked that gauge at you."

"Yeah, that was me, but wasn't no screaming, it was more like a manly yell," I replied with a hard look upon my face that I angrily held for a couple seconds.

Then I smiled away, and said, "Naw I'm just fucking with you. I was screaming like a bitch. I thought that officer was gone *kill me*, 'cause ain't no shot boxes outside."

And we laughed at my high-pitched screams that had allegedly echoed throughout the compound.

J-Rock was from some off-brand suburb that I don't care to remember. He was educated, clean, and displayed cell etiquette. Plus astrologically our signs met up; he was an Aquarius, just like me. So for the next two weeks we got along swell.

Click! *Click!* CLICK!

"Man it sounds like they deadlocking the doors. What time is it?" J-Rock said as he hastily moved to the bars, mirror in hand, to look down the gallery.

"It's 11:43 a.m.," I responded.

"Damn man, we on lockdown!"

Click! Click! Click!

"Hey, Officer Dickface, why we on lockdown?" J-Rock questioned the C/O.

"Something happened in the West House."

"WHAT?"

"They don't tell me shit, I just turn keys," Dickface responded and continued to deadlock the remaining cell doors.

"An officer got hit."

"Rasheed, how you know that?"

"That's the only time they keep they mouth closed. If something else happened, you gotta slap 'em to shut the fuck up about it."

J-Rock laughed and said, "You sholl right about that. How long you think we gone be on lockdown for?"

"That depends on how bad the officer got messed up, at the very least. You might as well get ready to kick back for thirty days."

"Damn man, my box low!"

"Who you telling? I smashed damn near everything playing catchup for all them months I was going back and forth to seg. I only got like fifteen noodles and a box of oatmeal pies left."

"I got you beat," J-Rock declared as he opened his property box and took inventory. "I got a case of noodles, four bags of beans and rice, two boxes of crackers, and a few wet packs."

"Oh you holding," I replied.

"Yeah, if we stay lockdown only thirty days, I'm straight."

"Even tho I don't have everything I want, I'm de-so too. I'm a just go into soldier mode and eat a half a noodle a day, 'cause they always serve hella slop whenever an officer gets scraped."

"Man, I ain't never realized that till you said something. I'm a start paying more attention 'cause I got fifty-two more years of this shit to deal with," J-Rock stated matter-of-factly.

"What you locked up for?"

"A murder."

"Oh, so all you gotta do is twenty-six straight before you go home," I voiced after doing the math.

"Naw, I'm not under fifty percent, I'm under the new law. I gotta do a hundred percent of my time. They maxed me out with sixty years, and I only been gone eight."

"Damn, I'm sorry to hear that," I responded as if he had just informed me about the death of a loved one.

Another young brother buried alive, buried alive.

"How you get so much time? What, they got your murder on video tape or something?"

Quick side note: The video tape comment was a slick way of asking, did he tell on himself?

"Naw. I got two rappies, one black and one white, and they both testified against me."

"I bet you the White boy broke first, didn't he?"

"Nope, it was my homie-homie since the third grade that tricked first."

"Damn, that's fucked up!"

"My White homie corroborated his testimony about a week before trial so they gave him thirty years at fifty percent instead of thirty years at a hundred percent."

"What they give your Black rappie then?"

"After he testified, gave his bitch ass a ride to the crib."

"*Wow!*"

The next twenty to twenty-five minutes, J-Rock dramatically shared with me everything that happened that fatal night like a well-trained thespian. When he finally finished, I asked, "You think you going to be able to give some of that time back?"

"Yeah, I got a clear-cut ineffective assistance of trial counsel claim, a boatload of prosecutorial misconduct, and a few other issues that I raised in my postconviction that got accepted by the appeals court."

"That's what's up."

Those three words came out of my mouth by habit but what I was thinking in my head was in total opposition of that statement.

J-Rock was a mixed breed. His mom was White and his father was Black. But despite being semiprivileged, he killed a White man in America. And on top of that, this White man was tragically shot while protecting his five-year-old baby girl, who rested soundly in the backseat of his vehicle during an attempted carjacking. So in the eyes of the law, J-Rock was blacker than three niggas. In addition, his two best friends fingered him as the trigger man. The reality of his whole situation: J-Rock will never see the streets again unless he can make it to his eightieth birthday. The odds of that happening with the rampant abuse of authority by correction officers, inadequate health care, unsanitary living conditions, a daily diet bombarded with *Soylent Green* (aka, soy meat), death of loved ones, family members and friends moving on with their lives, prison violence, institutional diseases, and a host of other stressors that come along with a penitentiary lifestyle—*good luck!*

I was just starting to feel sorry for him until he answered my next question.

"When you give that time back and get free, what's the first thing you gone do?"

"I'm a kidnap my first rappie that turned states on me and his daughter. She nine right now, she should be about fifteen when I give all this time back. Then I'm a handcuff him to a chair and chain her to a merry-go-round butt-ass naked that I'm a already have set up in my basement. Then I'm a gag him and rape his daughter right in front of him. And when she gets to crying, hollering, and begging me to stop, I'm a say, 'I ain't doing this to you, your daddy doing this to you.' Then I'm a get to spinning that merry-go-round, and every time she come back around to me, I'm a look her daddy in his eyes, pump back into her, and say, 'You see what you making me do, *huh? Huh?* You see what you making me do?' Then I'm a murk—"

I interrupted him mid-mayhem talk. I had enough of this descriptive and diabolically evil rape-murder scenario.

"J-Rock, what his daughter got to do with him telling on you?"

"I wanna hurt him the same way he hurt me, by getting me all this time."

"So why get down on his daughter? She ain't do nothing to you."

"I wanna defile and destroy what he loves the most, the same way that he defiled and destroyed my freedom when he got on that stand and testified against me."

This nigga was starting to really piss me off, so I changed the subject and never brought it up again. It's scary how the human mind can get so twisted that wrong becomes right and evil fair-seeming. And it is even more alarming to know that you can go completely insane and all the people that you come into contact with can see your insanity, all but you. How can that be fixed?

The word on the compound was that we would be on lock-down about thirty days because the officer did not get scraped too bad. Twenty-one days in, J-Rock woke me from a restful sleep and handed me a Western Union receipt.

"What time is it?" I asked as the light pierced the darkness of my eyelids.

"About 4:30 p.m."

In prison, a Western Union receipt is a printed-out piece of paper that shows the time and date that someone in the world wired you some lootchie. It also displays the full name of the person and the amount of money sent. Unfolding my printout, I saw that my mom sent me fifty bucks. Then I lay back down in an attempt to find that sweet spot that I had been awakened from.

"Hey, Rasheed?"

"What's up man?" I said, annoyed now by the second intrusion upon my rest.

"How much money you get?"

That question aggravated me even more because I knew he had looked at my receipt while I was sleeping. Why the fuck did Officer Dickface give him my mail, anyway? I did not want this fucking sicko knowing my mother's full name.

"I got fifty thousand dollars in nigga," I snidely responded.

"On the real, how much you get?"

"Fifty bucks man."

"That's how much I got," he responded with an elated tone.

58

Good for you, I sarcastically retorted in my mind, but I opted to remain silent.

Sensing my reticence, J-Rock said, "I'll holler at you when you get up."

"Naw, it's cool, I'm up now," I said as I rose to wash my face and brush my teeth.

"When you fill out your commissary slip, I want you to get some items for me and I'll grab you a couple extra boxes of those Nutty Bars you love so much and whatever else."

"That's what's up. Let me get myself together and we can do that in a minute."

In prison, commissary is everything. Commissary lines right up after safety, and sometimes your safety is listed on the same line as commissary, especially if you are paying punk fees. In the Pit, an inmate is allowed to spend as much money as he can at the commissary. Hooray! But there is a catch. Boo! In prison, there is always a catch. There are set limits for each item that you can purchase. So if you look at the item limit issue from a microlevel, inmate spending is actually controlled.

For example, we are only allowed to buy two boxes of Nutty Bars per inmate. So if I wanted two more boxes, I would have to find someone who does not eat Nutty Bars and have him buy the other two. Then in return, I would purchase some items for him that he would like extras of, at equal monetary value; understand? My name is Raylan Gilford, your penitentiary professor for today, and this is the Prison Barter System 101.

I have questioned many prison officials about the reason for commissary item limits, and the answer is always the same: "Gilford, there are about three thousand inmates in this facility. We set limits in commissary so every inmate can have access to what he needs."

That answer is a bunch of malarkey. All the commissary supervisors have to do is order larger quantities from their wholesale distributers. The fact of the matter is that commissary is used to control the prison population. You act "good," you get to go to commissary and eat semidecent. You act "bad," you eat the slop they feed you or starve. This control system would be ideal if only the rule breakers were punished, but even the inmates who follow the rules are locked down just like the infractors. It's my money; I should be able to buy one hundred boxes of Nutty Bars if I choose, right? Wrong! Commissary is a privilege, not a constitutional right. Does that seem fair to you? I think commissary should be a constitutional right and not a privilege, because technically I am a ward of the state and I pay state taxes on all the items that I purchase.

Moreover, in Menard, whenever your gallery goes to the store, your name has to be on the officer's commissary list. If your name is absent from that list, you are not allowed to leave the cell and cannot shop. Why? Your Inmate Trust Fund Account holds less than five dollars. So in the eyes of the administration, you are considered broke, even if all you wanted to buy was a couple of bars of soap to wash your ass. Yes, the IDOC overflows with empathy.

I would always keep a fin ball on my books to ensure my name stayed on that officer's commissary list because my family members, loved ones, and friends would wire me a few dollars whenever they could.

As proposed, thirtysomething days later we came off lockdown, and even though it was raining outside the sun was shining brightly upon the East Cell House because we were allowed to go to commissary first.

"J-Rock, wake up, we off lockdown. As soon as count clear, they running nine and seven gallery to store first."

"Quit playing man," he grouchily retorted and pulled the sheet over his head.

"All right."

About twenty minutes passed, then we heard the undeadlocking of cell doors, and Officer Dickface yelled repeatedly at the top of his lungs, "Get up and get ready for commissary! Get up and get ready for commissary!"

J-Rock jumped up and began getting dressed hurriedly while I laughed out loud at his comedic, one-man rendition of the Three Stooges.

"I told you," I said while chuckling.

"Fuck you," he angrily retorted.

"Man your breath gone smell like correctional sex in the commissary."

"No it ain't," J-Rock declared as he squeezed a gang of toothpaste in his mouth and squished it around.

"Both you guys are on the commissary list. If you going, be ready when I come back," Officer Dickface announced with authority as he continued to inform the rest of the gallery about their financial status. J-Rock and I talked all the way to commissary and all the way back. We were both elated by the prospect of being able to eat something other than semicold mashed potatoes, over prepared mixed vegetables and undercooked mystery meat.

"Man, they had everything over there," J-Rock said as he sat his bag of commissary down.

"I know. I wish I had some more lootchie," I responded as I opened my property box and began stacking my ramen noodles.

"How much of your money did you spend?"

"Everything. Fifty-four dollars, thirty-seven cents," I said as I looked at my commissary receipt.

J-Rock mugged me the same way that Scarface mugged Manolo when he caught him with his baby sister. Then he handed me the rest of my items that he purchased for me and soon after said, "Hurry up and give me my shit," with his tone matching his demeanor.

At first, I was taken aback. *What the fuck just happened?* was all I was thinking. *Wow.* An atmosphere that was once clear of all the bullshit was now riddled with malice and resentment. I could not begin to tell you why. For a minute I was about to ask him, *J-Rock, what's wrong? What I do?* But fuck that; ain't no psycho finta have me feeling like a battered husband. So I mugged up in kind and threw what I purchased for him upon his bed.

Nine months straight, we exchanged no additional giggles nor shared anymore laughs. Real talk: the only time we spoke was to inform the other of a lavatory situation. I totally disliked our new way of life. Maximum-security prison is frosty as fuck, but it hits hypothermic levels in no time at all when the person you live with acts as if you do not even exist. Abraham Maslow was not lying when he placed love and belonging in the third slot of his hierarchy of needs, right after basic human needs and safety.

Some days, when my people-pleasing desire tried to overpower me, I would just tell myself, why the fuck do I want to be bosom buddies with a wannabe pedophile/rapist? And that pleasing predisposition would dissipate in no time at all. But in the back of my mind, I would always wonder, why we beefing? A few more quiet-storm months passed before I received an answer to that pestering question.

The whole prison had been impatiently waiting to see the movie *The Wash* starring Dr. Dre and Snoop Dogg, and Eminem making an appearance. They finally rented that joint and it was programmed to play at 7:00 p.m. throughout the entire facility on the institutional movie channel. About 5:30 p.m., I was shaken by a loud noise. *Boo-boom!*

"Damn man, my TV blew out!" J-Rock screamed as he unplugged his television and attempted to figure out what was wrong. That blast startled the shit out of me, so I had a feeling that his TV was not coming back on.

"Damn, I'm a miss the movie. Damn I'm a miss the movie. Damn I'm a miss the movie," Was all J-Rock kept saying as he labored to fix his television.

After hearing him struggle for over an hour, I finally jumped down and said, "Man, you welcome to watch the movie with me. I got a double jack. We can both plug our headphones in."

"Hell yeah," he sheepishly responded.

FYI: After the year 1999, a large percentage of the televisions sold throughout the Illinois Department of Corrections were sold without speakers. Meaning, if you wanted to listen to your newly purchased fourteen-inch, $206.19 color television, you had to use headphones because the speaker was removed beforehand by the prison administration. Do you think that it is fair for an incarcerated man or woman to pay above market price for a fourteen-inch color TV minus a speaker?

Any right-minded person would say the price of the television should be lowered if parts are removed, or at the very least the incarcerated purchaser should be allowed to mail the speaker home because he or she paid for it. You in the free world as a consumer can go to another store if you do not like the removal of parts or the price of a product. Where can I go to receive all the parts that I pay for at a competitive price? There is only one store in my world. Right is right, and wrong is wrong. But when it comes to the administrative policies of IDOC, even when they're dead wrong, they're right. Please help us.

J-Rock placed his TV on the floor and moved mine to the bottom bunk nightstand. I opened my property box, handed him the double jack, and he plugged us in.

"I really do appreciate this Rasheed."

"Aw man, it ain't nothing."

"Did you hear my TV when it blew out?"

"Hell yeah, I jumped like I was in the world getting shot at again."

"You should've seen me. I almost ran through them bars like on the cartoons."

We laughed, bonding over the trauma one would experience growing up in an impoverished neighborhood.

"I'm finta hook up some burritos real quick before the movie start. You hungry?" I asked.

"I'll pass. Letting me watch the tube is good enough."

"Man, don't be shy now. If you hungry, let's eat."

"Yeah, let me get one."

"We already went through all that when I first moved in the cell. Ain't no one burrito gone do nothing for you. You can eat my food and still don't talk to me. I ain't proud."

And that joke opened the floodgates because we laughed like old friends who had been separated for years by an ocean of pain.

Now, some of you may be wondering how J-Rock and I went from enemies to best friends all within a blink of an eye. Look at it this way: when you are trapped in a cell with another man for twenty-three hours, five days a week, and twenty-one hours a day for the other two, all you got is each other. It's kind of like being stranded on a deserted island with a complete stranger; you two will become friends, eventually fall out about something, but best believe you will be friends all over again because isolation is a bitch. If you think I'm lying, lock yourself in a room with two TVs, two beds, food, and an adjoining bathroom with a complete stranger for thirty days. I guarantee y'all are going to become friends, mortal enemies, and best friends all over again within that little time spent together. Maslow, remember?

"How you still got food?" J-Rock asked. "We ain't been to the store in over a month."

"I saved some specifically for this movie," I said.

"Damn!" J-Rock yelled as I pulled a plastic bag full of commissary from my property box. "How you keep all that?"

"I put this bad boy all the way in the back in the corner with clothes on top so I wouldn't think about it," I said, smiling.

I opened the bag and slowly pulled out two summer sausages, three noodles, cheese, a bag of BBQ corn chips and a pack of tortilla shells. I hooked the burritos up and split everything down the middle with moments to spare. The movie *The Wash* was off the chain. We chomped down and laughed away.

When the film ended, we talked about our favorite scenes and rehearsed the new jokes we just learned. Since it was such a festive occasion and J-Rock seemed to be so open, I decided to ask what we were beefing about. I just had to know.

"J-Rock, we could have been kicking it like this every day man. What happened?"

He looked at me and opened his mouth as if he was about to tell me the problem, then he shut down and turned away.

"Come on man, what's up?" I voiced in a pleading manner.

"You spent more money than me," he said with a stern look on his face.

"What you talking about?"

"When we went to commissary, after that first lockdown, when you just moved in."

I had to think hard because I honestly could not remember or understand what the fuck he was talking about. Then I traced back in my mind the very first time that he had mugged me.

"*Awww*, I know what you talking about. I spent fifty bucks that day, but you spent fifty too, right?"

"Yeah, but you spent fifty-four, thirty-seven."

"Wait, *what?*"

My head exploded as I tried to wrap my mind around what he had just said. To make sure that he was talking about what I thought he was talking about, I said, "That extra fin ball I spent is what I usually keep on the books to get out the cell."

"Yeah, I know. But you still spent more than me."

This envious piece of shit waged war against me for a whole year because I spent a few more dollars than him. *Fucking prison.*

As I contemplated the lunacy, J-Rock caught me completely off guard when he said with an apologetic look, "I was trippin', man, my bag."

"You're forgiven," I said with a smile, using an authoritarian voice as I drew a cross in the air like I was a Catholic priest absolving him of his sin.

We both laughed and continued to kick the boe-boes about the movie until the wee hours of the morning.

Honestly, I did not forgive J-Rock. I just said what needed to be said to keep the peace in a psychotically hostile environment. In the Pit, if you got a bug for a cellmate, the correctional officers will not move you to a new cell because the prison is filled to capacity. This overabundance of inmates stems from that new 85–100 percent law passed in 1997 for violent offenders. Nobody is going home now, so it makes it even harder to move or breathe in prison. With that being said, you got one of two options: protective custody or physically fight to be separated.

For me, PC is definitely out the question because I would have even less movement outside the cell than I have now in general population. Why? The C/O's do not want to work as it is. So if I have to be physically protected wherever I go throughout the institution, then I would not be going anywhere. We could knuckle up and then go to segregation. But I could end up in seg or when I return to GP with a cellie worse than J-Rock. So I decided to stay with the devil that I know.

When I heard J-Rock snoring, I knew he was sound asleep. So I search through my property box and found that year-old commissary receipt. Guess what? This jealous motherfucker remembered the exact amount of money I spent: $54.37. I ain't gonna lie, that shook the shit out of me, so for the rest of the time that we lived together, I fake-laughed at all his jokes. And I was very mindful of the things that I would say and do around him. But most importantly, without fail, I never spent more money than him at the commissary, even when I had more money to spend. I stayed well below his psychotic financial radar.

Some people might read this and say I got punked out. Well, the Bible says, "A wise man foresees evil and hides himself," and I was hiding like a motherfucker. Ain't no nigga finta kill me in my sleep over some zoo-zoos and wam-wams. *Fuck commissary!*

What would you do if you were me?

BONUS CHAPTER

The Effects of PTPSS

A large percentage of Illinois prisoners suffer from Progressive Traumatic Prison Stress Syndrome, a term coined by leading, self-appointed penitentiary psychologist Raylan Gilford. PTPSS is defined as exposure to overwhelming fear or repetitive episodes of fear, deemed violent by the incarcerated individual, whether real or imagined.

"Violence" to PTPSS sufferers includes but is not limited to slamming cell doors, yelling correctional officers, inadequate protection, overwhelming stress, and the daily threat or the actual experience of physical and/or sexual abuse. If left untreated, PTPSS can have adverse short-term and long-term effects upon an individual's mental, spiritual, physical, emotional, sexual, subconscious, moral, and intellectual development.

As much as I hated all five of those jerks who psychologically scarred me, perhaps for the rest of my life, they're still my incarcerated comrades. And you would be crazy too if you experienced a fraction of the things that we've been through. So for the sake of equality, to show you that I'm not as white as snow; let me tell you a little story about myself when I went crazy for a minute.

A caramel-complected, five-foot-nine, hundred-eighty-pound, twenty-nine-year-old Black man with boyish good looks enters the scene. Hey y'all; it's me, Rasheed (smile). This incident took place back in 2005, so I was still staying in the East House cell 720.

In prison, one day rolls into another, and your daily routine becomes more of just the same old, same old. So if anything new or out of the ordinary takes place, it's talked about for days on end.

Case in point, Menard's commissary began selling bit-sized strawberry cookies. You know, the miniature joints, and I could not wait to load up on them. The cookie limit was six bags, so I maxed out when I went over there. And I had someone else snatch me up six more bags. So I was locked and loaded. I went eleven whole years without the sweet taste of strawberries resting upon my palate. It felt so good to have that delightful treat inside my mouth once again, even if it was in cookie form. I smashed two bags in the door, boom-boom. Then I started on my third bag and bit the right side of my cheek hard as hell.

Fuck! I screamed in my head as tears welled up in my eyes.

A good situation just turned bad, all bad. A mouth that was once filled with sweet, fruity deliciousness now tasted like a rusty penny.

Stop eating like a wild animal! chided my subconscious mind.

I was unable to eat past the pain and the bloody taste that was pouring into my mouth from an injured jaw. So I closed up my bag of goodies and lay back in the bed madder than a bitch.

While in Menard, for reasons unbeknownst to me, we were never allowed to walk over to the chow hall for breakfast, only lunch and dinner. So every morning like clockwork, we would happily receive penitentiary room service. I rarely ate the breakfast trays because the oatmeal, eggs, or whatever else would be served cold as fuck. However, I did enjoy drinking the juice and semicold milks that came along with the food.

Night turned into predawn, and I was awakening once again by the soul-nourishing rhythmic chant of Abdul Aziz, my brother and friend calling the adhan. Most inmates are sound asleep around this time of morning, so his soothing voice echoed throughout the East Cell House, signaling to all the believers far and wide that it was time to perform the Fajr prayer.

I woke up, washed my face and teeth, performed wudu, and then performed salat. After prayer, I read my Holy Quran for a while and meditated upon some of the mercies of Allah. While contemplating, a small, still voice from within whispered, "Just like all good things have to come to an end, likewise, all bad things have to come to an end, so stay strong soldier."

And with that, I laced up my Nikes and prepared for the day.

I sat my breakfast tray to the side for my cellie, who was still resting at the time. I swallowed a four-ounce 100 percent apple juice in two glops. As I removed the eight-ounce milk cartons from the bars, *bing!* I got a bright idea. I pulled out my bowl, grabbed a plastic spoon, and reopened that third bag of strawberry cookies that I wrecked my jaw on the other day. I crunched those miniature cookies up into even smaller pieces then poured them into my bowl, splashed some milk on top of them bad boys, and dug in. *Crunch Berries, Crunch Berries, Crunch Berries cereal!* I sang in my head as I ate away on the left side of my mouth.

This taste took me back, way back. I felt like a kid again on a Saturday morning sitting at my mother's kitchen table, feet swinging, as I enjoyed the sugary sweetness of Cap'n Crunch Berries cereal.

Before I knew it, I was on my fourth bag as the intoxicating nostalgia of home and Saturday morning cartoons consumed me. I couldn't believe how much these joints tasted like Crunch Berries. The only difference being I had to eat 'em real fast before the milk dissolved the strawberry cookies into nothing.

By the time I opened my fifth bag of cereal, I was silently humming, dancing, and carefully breaking those miniature cookies in half. When I filled the bowl to the top this time around with my penitentiary Crunch Berries, I poured the last of my milk on top and crunched away. Two spoonfuls later, I got the bubble guts. *Bloop-bloop.*

Fuck me! I said in my head while rushing to hang a sheet at the edge of the bed to obstruct the view of the toilet from my resting roommate and vice versa. As I covered the cold steel commode with toilet tissue, I thought about how my Crunch Berries would turn into a watery mush and crunch no more by the time I finished defecating.

I have never been the type of person who had trouble with multitasking. So I sat on the toilet with my cereal in hand and I ate and shat all at the same damn time. No bullshit, I would flush and chomp, flush and chomp, flush and chomp away. And all was right and felt good in my world.

I didn't realize that I had gone completely insane until Officer Dickface walked by with his clipboard for the 7:00 a.m. inmate count. He glanced at me on the toilet and my sleeping cellmate. Officer Dickface was about to check us off the clipboard until out of nowhere he did a double take and swung his head back in my direction. We locked eyes as I held a bowl in one hand and a spoonful of cereal in the other. My feed hole was wide open as he caught me in the midst of another mouthwatering bite. My eyeballs were bugged like a crazy-ass deer that got caught in front of some highway headlights shitting and eating Crunch Berries cereal at the same damn time.

Officer Dickface looked at me with a facial expression that was filled with so much disgust that he smacked me back to reality. And he held that more-than-understandable look for at least ten seconds before he just shook his head in disbelief and continued on with his daily routine.

I was so embarrassed and ashamed of that insanely intimate moment Officer Dickface and I shared that I dropped two more turds and ate what was left in my bowl like I was in a pie-eating contest. *Eeew!* Naw, I'm just fucking with you. I immediately placed the spoon in my bowl and sat everything on the floor in front of me. On the real though, after that shitty situation, I could no longer look Officer Dickface in his eyes. And whenever he would walk my way, I would just hold my head down or turn away.

He should have gotten a raise, hazard pay, or something for having to see some literal shit like that. Some things in life you can never unsee; they stay with you forever, and that was one of them.

Officer Dickface, I'm sorry you had to witness my Brookfield Zoo moment. But in my defense, it was the deprivation of strawberries and my PTPSS driving me crazy.

All jokes aside. Progressive Traumatic Prison Stress Syndrome is no laughing matter. PTPSS is something that I struggle with every day, as do many of my incarcerated comrades. We need some help. We need your help.

What would you do if you were we?

In conclusion, over the last twenty-six years of my life, I have obtained several degrees. I received a penitentiary degree in cellie day-care, drug rehabilitation, and prison psychology from the Almighty University of Incarceration. Without mastery of said achievements in penal academia, I would probably be in a coffin or boxed in a cell forever. So I wanna thank the Creator of the very first human mind for guidance, protection, and for placing the proper people and books in my path to improve upon my manhood.

Mr. Steve Sherman, my writing coach, would always say while critiquing my writing, "Gilford, trust your narration." And I would always respond, "I understand." Honestly, I still don't know what the fuck he was talking about. I am a victim of the Chicago Public Schooling System. Meaning, I did the best that I could with the few tools I possess. And I want to say to all of you academically trained writers who spent many woman hours in the lab studying and perfecting your craft, sorry for being such a hack.

The underlying theme of this book is one of prison reform. No big words, no acronyms, and no funding needed; just six words: "STAY THE FUCK OUT OF PRISON!"

The Department of Corrections does not correct a motherfucking thing. The DOC isn't designed to correct behavior. It's geared to manage and control violent behaviors. Life is a series of serious choices. Never forget, it always boils down to individual choice, so choose wisely.

Glossary/Prisonary

Allah. The Creator of the heavens and earth
adhan. The call to prayer for Muslims
akhi. Brother, friend
Alhamdulillah. "Praise God"
ancient city of Kemet. Ancient Egypt
As-salam alaykum. "Peace be upon you"
beefing. Into it with each other; a disagreement; physical fight; verbal or nonverbal confrontation
bird bath. To wash your whole body with soap and water in a sink like a prostitute
bit. The time you spend in prison
boe-boes. Having a conversation; talking; reminiscing with someone
BO. Body odor; bad smell; funk
bootie. Derriere; gluts; gluteus; buttock; ass
bootie bandit. A sexual predator that rapes men in prison
boyz. Homeboys; homies; friends
broke. Snitch; told; police informant
bubble guts. Gotta take a shit; defecate
bug. A crazy person; psych patient
butt naked. Wearing nothing
came up. Received something good
catch-22. Damned if you do and damned if you don't; a trap either way
'cause. Short for the word *because*
cell etiquette. To have respect for your cellmate; for example, you make as little noise as possible while your roommate is sleeping
cellie. Roomie, bunkmate, cellmate
Chi-Town. Short for Chicago

chow. What breakfast, lunch, and dinner is called in prison

commissary. The prison store where electronics, food, hygiene items, shoes, and clothes are sold

Congregational salat. More than one Muslim praying together

convict. Someone who lives by the rules created by the prisoners; for example, you never snitch

cooties. What children say other kids have when they itch uncontrollably due to filth or a rash

coppers. Correctional officers; police; the authorities

correctional sex. Homosexual lovemaking in prison

C/O's. Short for correctional officers

crib. House, home, comfort zone

cuzo. Short for cousin

Daniel-san. Ralph Macchio aka Danny LaRusso from the original *Karate Kid* movie

dap. To shake hands by bumping fists

DDT. Devastatingly violent wrestling move created by Jake the Snake Roberts

de-so. Decent; all right; okay

dookie. Feces; fecal matter; defecation

dressed. Kicked his ass; beat him up; stomped him out

D-Town. Short for Decatur

fajr. Morning prayer, the first of five daily prayers for Muslims

fat boyishly. To eat like a hungry fat kid

fin ball. Five American dollars

finta. I'm about to; I'm going to

fo. For

fracking. Used instead of the word *fucking* in the remake of the television series *Battlestar Galactica*

free world. Civilization outside of prison

get down. Hurt; attack; harm

gonna. "Going to"

gotta. Got to; have to

GP. The general population in prison

HAM. Acronym for "Hard Ass a Motherfucker;" to go wild or crazy

hella. A lot; extra; abundance

helluva. A whole lot; overabundance

Holy Quran. Religious book for Muslims

Homie-homie. Best friend; right-hand man; blood brother

hole. Segregation in prison

hood rage. The anger and trauma that builds up inside a person growing up in an impoverished environment

impoverishenza. An inferior state of mind one would have after being raised in a poor and violent culture; the opposite of affluenza

infractors. The rule breakers

in the door. Immediately; first

Iron Man. Hard, strong, and impervious; the material that *Marvel Comics* superhero Iron Man's suit is made of

joint. Thing or penitentiary

Joker smile. A fake smile like the painted face of Jack Nicholson and Heath Ledger in the Batman movies

knuckle up. To physically fight

kryptonite. An out of this world metamorphic crystal that weakens DC Comics hero Superman

Kush. Nubia, ancient region in Africa

lootchie. Money; cash; dinero

man meat. Dick; penis; "sword"

mug. To make an angry or fighting face

mugged up. War face; to hold a violent facial expression

murder weapons. Guns

murk. To murder; kill; destroy

my bag. "I'm sorry;" "I apologize"

naw. No

nigga. An ignorant person or friend

no talk. To refuse to talk to someone

'nother. Another

off brand. Anything not Chicago or generic

outta. Out of

PC. Protective custody in prison, not part of the prison general population; inmates who fear for their safety and are housed separately

penitentiary etiquette. To respect everyone's person, property, and space in prison

penitentiary rage. Anger that boils inside a person from the trauma one experiences during long-term incarceration

police-ism. To support the authorities in everything they do; to honor the Blue Code even though you are an ordinary citizen or inmate

prison lingo. The language that prisoners use and the meaning of those words

psychological cell games. Mental, spiritual, and emotional mind games used to control a weaker cellmate

punked out. Embarrassed; made to look weak; scared; have your manhood taken

punk fees. Paying for protection in prison; being extorted

Ramadan. The ninth month of the Islamic calendar, during which Muslims all around the world abstain from food and drink from sunrise till sunset

rappies. People who commit a crime together

ronin. A masterless samurai

rule one. To mind your own business in prison

salat. A specific way to perform prayer for Muslims

Scarface'ly. To look, talk, or act like the lead actor Tony Montana in the 1983 movie *Scarface*

scrape. To beat up; to physically hurt or injure a person

seg. Short for segregation, the place where inmates who break the institutional rules are housed

sho. "Sure"

sholl. "Sure is"

shook. To be scared; frightened

smashed. Ate up; devoured; or to beat up someone

sneak thief. An inmate who steals from other prisoners

soldier mode. To act as a military soldier; to be unemotional during the process of completing a mission to survive and defend

Soylent Green. A 1973 movie starring Charlton Heston (spoiler alert!) about a cop who discovers that human beings are being processed into a mysterious synthetic food

steal on. To punch an unsuspecting person in the face

stunt. Lying; boasting; showing out

swag. To walk, talk, dress, and act in a way that is admired by others

swiller. Dick; penis

taqwa. God consciousness; to make right decisions as if God is sitting next to you or at the very least carry yourself as if you know that God is watching everything you do

titties. Female breast

thang. Thing

that's what's up. Okay; I agree

the Pit. Nickname for Menard Correctional Center

the Sweet Science. The sport of boxing

the world. Society or anything that is off prison grounds

tho. Though

tube. TV

trippin'. Made a mistake; went crazy

turned down. To calm down; to get control over oneself

turned states. To testify in a court of law for the state prosecution; to snitch; rat out someone

Walaykum as-salam. "And peace be upon you"

wax on and wax off. To use circular motions like Danny LaRusso when he waxed Mr. Miyagi's cars in the original 1984 *The Karate Kid* movie

wet dreams. Semen emission during REM sleep

wet pack. A sealed, single-serving container of food that holds vittles such as tuna, chili, and pork

White nigga. An ignorant or nasty White man

whoopin'. Getting your ass kicked; beat down

wudu. A cleansing process performed by Muslims before prayer

zoo-zoos and wam-wams. Cakes, cookies, and chips

yard bird. Chicken

you feel me? "Understand?" or "Do you agree?"

402 Conference. To talk it out with someone; to come to a peaceful resolution or agreement when you don't want any trouble

How to Survive in Prison

12 Rules

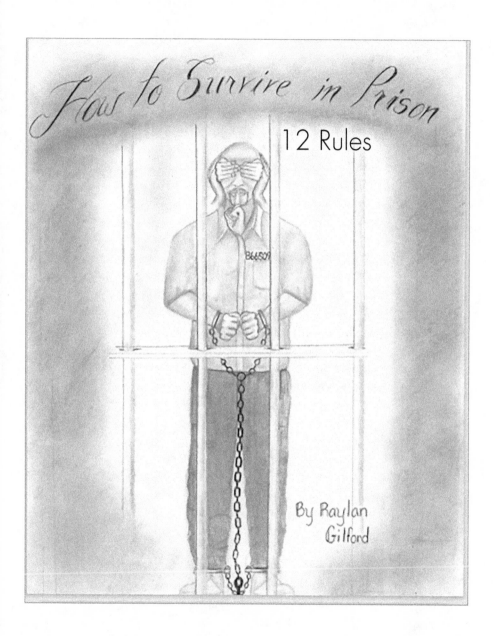

By Raylan
Gilford

Contents

Introduction

True knowledge is increasing a person's
view or perspective, in spite of...
—Raylan Gilford

Ray, Ray-Ray, Shorty Four, and Lil Killer are some nicknames that various peers of my carceral experience had called me at some point in time. My mom and dad christened me Raylan Gilford. Today I prefer to be called Abdul-Rasheed.

There is a lot that comes with a person's name. A name is more than just haphazard letters thrown together to address an individual. A name has meaning that can express your character, personality, being, heritage, bloodline, heart, and soul.

Let's use "Raylan" for example. I was named after both of my uncles/godbrothers (don't ask). One of my uncles' middle names is Ray and the other's first name is Landon. My mom, with her infinite love for the two, placed those names together and created Raylan.

Now my Uncle Ray is a hardworking, college-educated, law-abiding, average, everyday citizen. My Uncle Landon is on the opposite end of life's spectrum. He's a gangster for real, a street dude, and the realest nigga I have ever known.

Juxtaposed, these two individuals could summarize my personality in a nutshell for about the first eighteen years of my life.

Unlike Uncle Ray. I never gave school or a nine-to-five job 100 percent of me. Likewise, as opposed to my Uncle Landon, I never invested all of me in the streets. Within both arenas, I did just enough to get by, enough to survive.

I walked that thin line between the civilian world and the street-life world, and I never truly felt like I belonged to either one. Plainly put, I was 50 percent Uncle Ray and 50 percent Uncle Landon, strangely mixed; hence the name Raylan.

Abdul-Rasheed is the name that was both given to me and also one that I chose for myself upon my reversion back to Al-Islam.

The name Abdul denotes a slave or servant of God. Rasheed means conscious, piety, or one who shows the straight way. No longer a fifty-fifty man, for the last twenty-three years of my life I have become a 100 percent conscious and pious servant of God who shows the straight way.

And that straight way for today is a "How to Survive in Prison" manual.

- Do you break the law? Are you thinking about doing something criminal?
- Have you ever used your five-finger discount at a grocery, department, or clothing store?
- Do you drink and drive?
- Have you ever texted while driving?
- Are you selling or using illegal drugs?
- Do you have unresolved anger issues?
- Are you mentally unbalanced and refusing to take your meds?
- Is there a family member, loved one, or friend making life choices that could land him or her inside a jail cell?

If you answered "yes" to any of those questions and you are unwilling to stop, change, seek professional help, or follow the laws of the land, then this book is for you.

I have been incarcerated within the Illinois Department of Corrections for the last twenty-six years of my life. Over the years of this life-threatening, skin-crawling, and fright-filled journey, only one thing has remained constant: my determination to survive.

Today, I am forty-five years of age, and if you do the math, it's clear that I have spent the majority of my life inside a prison compound. I'm not ashamed to admit that prison and doing time is all that I know.

During this arduous imprisonment, I have witnessed so many brutal and heinous things that I can never unsee. Some days, these violent images get stuck on replay at the forefront of my mind. Then when you add on top of those mental events all the ungodly things I have had to do to remain whole, it's short of a miracle that I haven't gone bat-shit crazy and started eating dookie out the toilet by now.

Real talk: I have survived multiple years inside some of Illinois's most savagely ruthless prisons. During that time, I have never been raped, stabbed, extorted, or beat too badly that I wasn't able to recover. I am a survivor in every sense of the word. It is safe to say that my penitentiary IQ is borderline genius.

The carceral knowledge stored within the pages of this book is much more practical than a doomsday manual, nuclear explosion survival kit, or a zombie apocalypse preparation pamphlet. How so? America, "the land of the free," has the highest incarceration rate of the entire industrialized world. So it's more than likely that an acquaintance, a close friend, a family member, or even *you* will land inside a jail cell before any of those mentioned disasters ever take place.

Can you survive?

How will you survive?

Contained within this "How to Survive in Prison" manual are twelve simple rules that you can use as a billboard-sized wooden guidepost or a flashing neon-green lighthouse to prevent you from getting lost inside any municipal county jail or the Illinois Department of Corrections.

Full disclosure: every rule and personal example spoken of in this book may be a complete fabrication, 'cause we all know you can't trust the antisocial ramblings of a convicted felon/criminal mind… can you?

Moreover, the violence that takes place in prison is not always predictable. These twelve rules do not guarantee your safety. They are not absolutes. But my rules will decrease the odds of you being brutally beaten, stabbed, raped, or even killed.

Read the writing on the walls.

Read the writing on the walls…

RULE 1

Mind Your Own Business

In prison, the preeminent rule of survival is minding your own business. If you want to stay alive, you *must* live like the three monkeys on a totem pole; you hear nothing, see nothing, and speak nothing.

Now, I am not telling you to be unaware of the things that are happening around you. I would never advise you not to pay attention, because to be aware is to be alive.

So for clarity, let me give you a short illustration on how to properly mind you own business within an incarcerated setting.

Say for instance you have two guys secretly discussing an issue about some illegal drugs, and you just so happen to be within hearing range of their conversation. You need to move the fuck around ASAP.

Why? Their stash spot can be raided at any time by prison officials. And if those drugs are found, guess who the suspected stool pigeon is going to be? Go ahead, guess.

If you guessed wrong, the assumed rat is anyone who was in listening range whenever the drug dealers discussed their illegal drug enterprise who just so happened to look like or maybe even act like an undercover cop.

The drug dealer's hasty, uneducated assumption makes a lot of sense, right? Of course it doesn't, but that is how some criminal minds work. Plainly put, somebody's got to get it, and you don't want your name to be on top of that short list.

Drugs are extremely hard to come by in prison, which makes them monstrously lucrative. In some correctional facilities, the profit margin of a hundred-dollar ounce of rego weed can earn you well over two thousand dollars in cash or commissary. And you can just imagine how much money the harder drugs are bringing in. So it should go without saying that the physical retaliation imposed upon the "alleged" informant is going to be brutal and heinous. Trust me, you don't want to be that guy. So whenever you are in earshot of any illegal activities, get the fuck out the way because your life depends on it.

In conclusion, just be aware that something major is being discussed and move around. Prison is like an overoccupied hamster's cage that has never been cleaned; eventually, the smell is going to get on you.

RULE 2

Mind Your Own Fucking Business

I cannot stress this enough: mind your own fucking business. You shouldn't give two bloody painful diarrhea shits about what someone else is charged with or how much time he may have to spend in prison. I don't care if he's a pedophile, rapist, or a pedophile-rapist-homosexual—so fucking what! That ain't your business. It's his and his alone.

Say you got a guy around you who incessantly brags about how much money he has on the street, but he always has his hands out for something to eat. Feed him or not but shut the fuck up about it.

Why? Let's just say Mr. Beggar is a bold-faced liar or he's rich as fuck but for whatever reason he can't get to his money. For the sake of this scenario, either one will do.

As Mr. Beggar spews his guts out about his financial portfolio, trust me, everyone inside of the pod is actively listening. Eventually someone or someones are going to take a bite at the monetary bait Mr. Beggar is dangling inside the stale correctional air.

The bait biters may decide to take care of all Mr. Beggar's needs while he's incarcerated. Then after being released from prison, Mr. Beggar will reimburse them tenfold. Once a verbal contract has been made between the two parties, protection of Mr. Beggar will reign supreme.

Finance 121: you got to protect your investment, right? So what do we have now? A vagabond with juice. Those of you who once laughed at him or talked bad about him to his face may become a victim of an old-fashioned ass whoopin'.

Fuck what everybody else says; "revenge is best served whenever it's served." So all Mr. Beggar has to do now is point, ask, and pay.

Most inmates in prison are not trained fighters. With that said, a simple beat-down can turn into a homicide faster than a fat bitch gliding down a Slip-N-Slide hilltop spattered with Johnson & Johnson baby oil. Believe me, you do not want to be the guy who gets accidentally killed over some childish, looking-down-your-nose-type bullshit, which could have been simply avoided by you shutting the fuck up.

But by all means, if you want to become a part of jailhouse folklore, run your mouth and you'll go down in history as "another guy" who lost his life in prison for violating rule 2.

Moving on, you shouldn't give two dirty dog dicks about what is being shown in another man's pictures. Unless he invites you to his family, those flicks are his escape portals and his alone.

And never, ever be concerned about what is being discussed on someone else's visit, phone time, or mail. As I stated before, unless he invites you into his world within a world, *mind your motherfucking business.*

Prison is geared toward stopping and changing violent and antisocial behaviors, publicly, within a carceral setting. Prison is not designed for privacy. You eat, sleep, shit, bathe, and breathe all day everyday under the watchful eyes of inmates and prison authorities.

So know for a surety, an inmate's pictures, visits, phone time, and mail are the closest he'll ever come to having something semi-tangible to being his own. Afford him that privacy because it may be your ass in a penitentiary sling if you don't.

This here is extremely important, so pay close attention. Not under any circumstance should you inquire about another inmate dealing in homosexuality. If he is chasing behind a punk for some boy booty, so fracking what! That's his business. *He's at risk for HIV/AIDS, not you.* So look the other way and keep it moving.

I can't even begin to tell you how many guys I have seen speak on some fag shit and get beat half to death over a geeche.

In the interest of transparency, look at it this way: in the hood, a nice percentage of wars are not over the blocks needed for illegal drug sales; that's ghetto propaganda. It's always over a bitch. A good-pussy-having, slow-blow-job-giving THOT. Stay with me now: in prison, the fags are the THOTs, understand?

Don't believe the TV; all punks ain't punks. You got some homo-thugs that are extremely violent when it involves correctional sex. So please hold your tongue 'cause them fun boys ain't playing.

Added bonus of gilla

Even correctional officers despise stool pigeons. Why? A nice percentage of them are doing illegal shit and riding dirty themselves. And we all know criminal minds think alike, regardless to what side of the carceral fence you may be standing on. So the po-po figure if you'll tell on a fellow inmate who is dealing with the same pressures of incarceration and who's under the same carceral restriction as you, push comes to shove, you'll trick on him.

Fifty thousand dollars a year with room for advancement, 401(k), full medical and dental, paid vacations, time and a half, double and triple pay on holidays and hazard pay, stupid-fat credit line, free haircuts, a sense of purpose, etcetera—them dirty bitches ain't trying to get their hands caught in the cookie jar and lose all that. They fucking hate you! But they utilize the stool pigeon because they know that snitches are a necessary evil to maintain order.

On the real, if you are known for speaking out of turn and you just so happen to witness something criminal and a choice has to be made between your physical safety or the dirty bopper losing his sweet-ass government job, best believe you're a dead motherfucker. He or she will discreetly set you out to the prison population as the snitch-bitch you are. *Bon voyage!*

In short, if you want to be seriously injured or maybe even killed, by all means be nosy. But know of a surety that you got something painfully life-changing coming your way. Now for those of you who want to survive imprisonment unscathed, never miss out on an opportunity to *mind your own fucking business!*

RULE 3

Respect, Respect, Respect...

Respect: to avoid violation of or interference with; a willingness to show consideration or deference. All the common courtesies that your parents instilled in you while growing up. Now for those of us who missed those valuable lessons, just utilize everything that Mr. Drummond taught Arnold and Willis on the thirty-minute hit TV sitcom *Different Strokes*. High-quality interracial humor; I know y'all were watching that shit.

In prison, the number one theme is RESPECT. That's what it's all about. Respect can and will carry you a long way inside any penal institution, I don't care who, if it's a hoe-boe, dope fiend, homosexual, or whatever—from the angriest midget to the giant simpleton, respect is due.

Respect, respect, respect…

For example, say two men are talking and you need the immediate attention of one of them. Don't just walk up and start speaking like what you got to say is more important than their discussion. Your blatant interruption is a form of disrespect and a quick way to get your lips split right down the middle. Have you ever had your lip creased like that? That shit hurt like a motherfucker every time you opened your mouth until it healed, didn't it?

Proper prison etiquette: Say something along these lines: "Excuse me, I don't mean to interrupt but…bla-bla-bla. Bla-bla-bla." Understand?

In another instance, say you have to walk between two men or a group of people who may or may not be talking at that moment. Try to walk around them. If that is not an option, do not—I repeat, do not—blow past 'em like you are the last real nigga alive. Those actions are a surefire way to get stabbed, beat the fuck up, or punched in the back of the head like Blue did in the 1998 movie *The Players Club.*

Proper prison etiquette: Say, "Pardon the body."

Those three small words will be a big contribution toward your physical wellbeing. And you can even duck your head down a little when you cautiously stroll through as an added touch of respect.

"Excuse me," "Pardon me," "My bag," "Sorry about that," "My fault" are words to live by, peace-building pleasantries that will carry you back through the doors of freedom. So please add these li'l respecties to your prison vernacular as soon as possible.

Added bonus of gilla

REM is an acronym for the term "rapid eye movement" to describe a certain kind of sleep. This unique form of slumber happens only when you are dreaming like an innocent little baby. Numerous sleep studies have unequivocally proven that when the rapid, periodic jerky movements of the eyes take place, you are in fact dreaming, hence the term "REM sleep."

Due to the noise level of various conversations, ignorant out-bursts from inmate and C/O's alike, rap battles, and the loud-voiced rambling of a psychotic mind, a good nap or eight blissful hours of sleep is extremely hard to come by in prison.

So when your cellmate is resting, please respect his sleep time by being as still as possible. Patiently wait for him to rise from his deep sleep before you start making noise. But if you just have to move around, glide as if you are an experienced-gay-cat-burglar on the prowl.

Joke aside, REM sleep is the only time that an incarcerated man can truly escape in accordance with the law from the confines of imprisonment. Let him be free to dream and feel the love of a good woman, hear the laughter of his children, or simply enjoy the travel-ing of an unanchored soul. Let him be free, and more times than not he'll afford you the same courtesy.

Moving along, I am admittedly not into any type of police-ism. So know of a surety that this lesson here is coming from a viewpoint of survival in prison and not from a position of being compliant with prison officials.

You must respect all correctional employees the same way that you respect your fellow inmates. Why? Well, for one, the police feed you your food when you are on lockdown. And two, generally speak-ing, correctional employees are here for your protection. And if you disrespect one of them for whatever reason, you better not ever need their assistance thereafter. Because you will clearly see their humanity take over when they turn their back on you in your time of need.

In addition, some boppers have worker-bee inmates on their payroll who readily do their bidding. These violent Stockholm syn-drome—suffering fools are paid with extra prison food, phone time, and various other petty penitentiary privileges. So disrespecting "that officer" is equivalent to disrespecting that brutally vicious mother-fucker standing right next to you. Always remember that respect is due on both sides of the prison fence.

Moreover, don't get it twisted: the police are the most dangerous gang inside of any correctional facility. So do not let their fake smiles and creased-up khakis fool you. And here's why:

1. In nearly all cases, they are the most organized mob.
2. They control all the guns and have the right to use deadly force whenever they see fit. Believe that!
3. They can extract you from your cell at any time, beat you to death, then hang you and write your murder up as another penitentiary suicide.

Yeah, your family may get paid thousands, even millions of dollars after the conclusion of a divinely inspired independent investigation. And the officers involved may even be suspended, laid off, or prosecuted to the fullest extent of the law. But how does that help you? You're deceased like a motherfucker, 'cause only Jesus Christ and Patrick Swayze in the movie *Ghost* came back from the dead.

Bottom line: respect is also due to them dirty bitches, if you want to come home alive.

Personal application of rules 1, 2, and 3

In 1995, Chicago, Illinois, I was housed in Cook County Jail, Division 9, North Tower, cell 2408.

When I walked on the deck for the first time, my homeboys pulled me to the side and introduced me to the rest of the clan. Then my main man explained to me the dos and don'ts and handed me a six-inch ice pick with a taped-up handle shaped like a Phillips head screwdriver.

As he and I proceeded to my new home away from home, a semihefty dude with pimp-like fingernails and a long, slicked-back perm grabbed the last of his property and exited the cell.

I cocked my head toward Mr. Slick-Back and my homeboy whispered, "He on the other side. He moving downstairs along the wall where they deep at."

"How deep?" I asked

"Like six to one."

"Fuck!"

"Yeah, now you see why I gave yo ass a banger in the door."

"I thought you were just being nice," I declared with a smile.

He looked me dead in my motherfucking eyes with the serious-ness of a man going to death row with a case pending and retorted, "If this deck go up, somebody gon' die, 'cause everybody got knives, even the Neutrons. I'm just trying to stop that shit from happening. But if it do, I want us to be on the giving end and far away from receiving."

To lighten the mood while attempting to lessen the thoughts of impending murder or death, I sang one of my favorite rap lyrics, "I promise I'll smoke chronic till the day that I die," smiling even harder.

"Man you always playing. Hurry up and get situated. I might be able to help you out with that," he retorted mildly as he walked away with a grin.

I swung open the cell door and there was this big, violent, Baby-Huey-looking-ass nigga standing at the back of the cell.

"My name Bear," he announced, breaking the silence.

"I'm sure it is," I said matter-of-factly affirming his nickname.

I slowly scanned my new quarters, searching for a good place to hide my sword.

"Bear, they call me Ray-Ray. You mind if I soap the cell up real fast?"

"That's cool, but it's already clean," he responded with a voice raspier than DMX.

I moved to the side and let his big ass step out the door. The first thing I grabbed was a brown paper bag that was sitting on the floor in the corner. I assumed it was trash, but all the paper inside was neatly stacked. I pulled out the contents and began to read.

It was a bag full of gang literature. That pimp-looking-ass nigga from the other side who had just moved out had left all his mob's paperwork.

Bear darkened the doorway.

"What you got there?"

"This ain't shit but some garbage man," I replied as I dropped the lit back in the brown bag and began to wipe the walls down.

When Bear turned his back again, I retrieved the gang lit from the bag and slid it under my bunk.

All throughout the night, I pondered what should I do with this shit. If I tore it up and flushed it down the toilet, sooner or later, Pimpin' Ken Cousin would realize it's missing and possibly remember where he left it. And that's me and Bear's ass in a penitentiary sling. How so you might ask? Six-to-one odds plus we don't know when it's coming equals a bloody mess. So I shook that intellection from my head.

I thought about showing the paperwork to my whole squad. But that would only bring war to our doorstep. Yeah, his kinfolk would have violated him for losing their gang literature. And used his face as a living example of a mistake you should never make while in jail. No bullshit, they would've beaten his head until it got as big as an overinflated medicine ball. Best believe your noggin can swell up like that. Indeed, a truly severe punishment for their so-called brother whom they allegedly "love."

Being labeled opposition, all Bear and I had to look forward to was death. Lord knows I ain't trying to die in a dirty, stinking county jail. So if I chose to display their business for the whole pod to see, the only choice I had left was to kill. I was nowhere near a killer. In fact, I was already charged with a murder and looking at sixty years of imprisonment. I was not trying to catch another body and, if convicted of both crimes, receive a natural life sentence. So I quickly aborted that thought as well.

Before daybreak, I decided to personally hand over the gang literature to its rightful owner.

Morning came, and I saw Mr. Perm chopping it up with one of his homeboys. I walked down the stairs, looking in his direction, as I cautiously approached their side of the pod. By the time our eyes met, I was about five feet away from him.

"Man I don't mean to interrupt, but can I holler at you for a minute?"

He touched his chest with his index finger and asked with a confused look, "Me?"

I nodded my head, and we walked over to the corner. I felt like everybody on the deck was watching us. But the two back walls and the angling of my body with his placed me in a position where only he could see what my fingers possessed.

As I slowly pulled their secret little words and bylaws from my pocket, his eyes got big as supersized-boe-dollars, and I handed everything over to him.

"Man you left this in my cell last night."

"Thank you, thank you, thank you man! What they call you?"

"Ray-Ray."

"Good looking, Ray-*Raaayyyy!*" he said, elongating my name while stomping his right foot.

"Ain't no big thang," I declared with a smile, then laughed at his pimpish ways.

He folded up the paperwork and put it in his pocket. We bumped fists, and I went back to my side of the town.

Personal application analysis

I respected his personal space as I approached him and his homeboys.

I respected his literature/personal property by not throwing it away or exposing it to my crew.

And I respected him enough to return to him what was rightfully his.

Respect, respect, respect…(rule 3)

Most importantly, not only did I mind my business (rule 1) but I minded my motherfucking business and kept it moving once I placed the paperwork back in his hands (rule 2).

I'm alive today, testifying that my system works in real-life penitentiary scenarios.

Quick side note: A couple of weeks down the line, Pimpin-Pimpin got a job working in Division 9 County Jail Inmate Commissary. No matter how much money I spent, I always came back to my cell carrying an extra-big commissary bag. You feel me!

RULE 4

Act Mad

Whenever you enter a new deck, wing, or facility, you should act as if you are "mad as fuck." If you are not good at pretending, just think about something that pissed you off in the past and hold that thought. Your facial expression and negative vibe should keep most predators at bay. But be ready, because eventually someone is going to ask you prison's most proverbial question, "What you locked up fo?"

When you reply, don't act hard, don't act tough. Act mad and simply say something to this effect:

"I'm pissed off right now man. I'll holler at you about that shit later." And leave it at that.

The majority of the inmate population will respect your answer because they have experienced firsthand those same feelings of deg-radation when their own oh-so-sweet American liberties were judi-ciously snatched away.

Moreover, that vexed feeling could be the nagging sound of your subconscious mind condemning acts that may have led to your incarceration:

Why you do that dumbass shit?

I told you not to!

Man, you done fucked up your life.

In addition, those riled-up feelings could be a scolding voice talking down to you from the other end of that collect call as you plead for assistance in your time of need.

Are you stupid?

You think money grow on trees?

I told you this was going to happen.

Further, that indignant feeling could be the stark, overwhelm-ing reality of your current predicament: senile fluorescent lighting, filthy MacNasty interior, an overused outhouse aroma, and being surrounded by society's rejects.

Most troubling, those infuriating thoughts could be the realiza-tion of you missing out on future birthdays, holidays, anniversaries, and family time. Or those disheartening feelings could be a traumatic cocktail of all the above.

What I am attempting to relate is that it is okay to be angry. Matter of fact, it is expected of you. So why not use this common reaction as an aid to secure your safety and survey the carceral terrain while taking a much-needed breather? Understand?

Now to appease the inmates who just have to know what your charge is, act mad as long as you can, then talk, because you have to share your offense. More times than not, these intrusive motherfuckers are not just being nosy for nosy's sake; they are also on the hunt for prison's most hated offenders: the pedophile and the rapist.

There's a story told in the New Testament of the Holy Bible of a woman who was about to be stoned to death for committing adultery (Old Testament Law). As the people of the town surrounded her with rocks, bricks, and boulders, Jesus Christ intervened on her behalf and said, "Let anyone who is without sin cast the first stone."

Guess what, ain't nobody throw shit. Why? The lesson being nobody is perfect. We all have indulged in some sinful shit at one point in time or another. Well, prison does not adhere to such a lofty standard of understanding. There is an unwritten hierarchy of status that is in direct correlation with your offense. And the rapists and pedophiles are at the bottom of this list:

Gang chief
Cop killer
Serial killer
Spree killer
Multiple murders
Double murder
Murder
Attempted murder
Drug dealer
Armed robbery
Kidnapping
Concealment of a homicide
Home invasion
Burglary
Auto theft
Theft
Forgery
Prostitution
Child abuse
Rapist
Pedophile

For the record, just so things don't get twisted, I'm at the top half of that list. I was charged and convicted of first-degree murder and concealment of a homicide. Now, I refuse to get into any particulars as to why rapists and pedophiles are hated with such passion. But in the interest of survival in prison, I'm a help you low-life motherfuckers out because some of you may actually be innocent in spite of being found guilty in a court of law.

So if you happened to be charged with a sexual assault or pedophilia, I suggest that you lie about your charge. And if you are convicted, make sure that the time you have (or say you have) lines up with the sentencing structure of one of the more respected offences. Then pray to the gods above that no one inquires about your crime through a third party from the Department of Corrections/Prisons Registry.

Furthermore, if you have a sexual assault or pedophilia case that is highly published and discussed on various news outlets: may God help you! And I urge you to check into PC as soon as possible because your physical, mental, and emotional wellbeing depends upon it.

Moving on. Once you inform the inquirer of your "respected offense," flip it on him real quick, and start asking questions about the legal system.

County jail example questions:

✓ How much time do these charges carry?
✓ You ever been locked up for this?

Penitentiary example questions:

✓ What kind of motions can I file to get back in court?
✓ Do you know somebody who can help me?

Most people in prison just want to be heard and feel relevant after being trapped in a voiceless environment. Be attentive and actively listen; some information may be shared that you can actually use to better your situation, and then again it may all be huff. The point of the matter: he is doing all the talking. Which gives you time to breathe and ease your prison anxieties. Who knows, maybe you will make a penitentiary friend in the process.

In two words, act mad. *Act mad!* Because anger is an expected and well-respected prison norm.

RULE 5

Make Eye Contact

Whenever you engage in a conversation on the inside, always make eye contact. Regardless if this person is a prison official or a fellow inmate, look him or her directly in the eyes while you parley. Solid eye contact in prison displays confidence and strength, which is something that you may be lacking at the time as you adapt to your new environment.

Have you ever seen the movie *Stir Crazy* starring Richard Pryor and Gene Wilder? If you haven't, this classic comedy is a must-see before your stint in prison. But if you are already boxed in, here are a few cinematic cliff notes to support rule 5. Harry Monroe (Richard Pryor) and Skip Donahue (Gene Wilder) were tried and convicted of armed robbery and sentenced to serve twenty years inside a maximum-security penitentiary for a crime they did not commit. They were scared to death. So to mask their fear of incarceration, they went into that joint walking hard as hell with a gangster swag that was out of this world, talking about, "We bad. We bad. Yeah, *we bad!*"

This is what consistent eye contact vocalizes to your prison ecosystem:

"I am a bad motherfucker."

But be careful; you can go too far with the eye contact. Use this tactic only when you are conversing or actively listening to someone. Outside of engaging conversation, solid eye contact could be interpreted as a sign of disrespect. "Smart eyeing" is what we call it.

Smart eyeing is where two men stare into each other's eyes, mug up, and whoever looks away first is "scared," and the victor is assumed "tougher" than the loser of this eye chicken game.

I cannot begin to tell you when this form of eye-boxing came into play. All I know is that it is goofy as hell and I never liked the shit. The only person whom I long to stare endlessly into my eyes is my lady. Like it or not, smart eyeing is a cornerstone of prison culture, so you better buck up.

Additionally, if your smart eyeing comes off as if you are a bad motherfucker in the wrong way as opposed to being a bad motherfucker in a good way (the *Stir Crazy* illustration), know that you do not want to be labeled a bad motherfucker unless you are truly a bad motherfucker. Why? Sooner or later, someone is going to try you just to see if what you are portraying is true.

Carceral fact: Everyone in prison, officers and inmates alike, will be tried and tested.

So to stay ahead of the game, if anyone attempts to smart eye you, look away, not in a fearful manner but as if you got something more important to focus on.

Personal application of rules 4 and 5

In September of 1998, I was transferred to Menard Correctional Center, a maximum-security prison located in Menard, Illinois. We approached the facility inside a piss-smelling, overcrowded prison bus filled with various classifications of extremely violent convicted felons. Panic filled my throat as the bus driver accelerated down a dangerously narrow winding hill not fit for speeds over ten miles an hour. And when the transporting vehicle swerved too close to the unencumbered edge, I braced myself for cliff-crashing impact by planting my shackled feet to the floor and snatching up against my handcuffed wrists that were locked to a junkyard dog chain that was tightly bound around my waist.

This bitch gone kill me! I hollered in my head as the other occupants unabashedly voiced their concerns. Screams, yells, and verbal threats went unanswered by the grinning driver as we swiftly descended about sixty feet into the ground.

I guess that's why Menard is aptly called "The Pit." It seemed as if someone took a heap of dynamite and blew a big-ass hole into the ground the size of a small town and built a penal institution inside that space.

The bus ride from Joliet Correctional Center to Menard Correctional Center took about twelve hours with only one rest stop in between. As the penitentiary gate locked behind us, we pulled in front of the prison chapel. I looked out the window and observed twenty emergency response team members (ERTM) standing in a straight line of ten and ten, facing one another, suited and booted in full riot gear with about four feet of space in between them. There was no doubt in my mind that this violent-looking-ass Soul Train line was an organized display of force and potential brutality. We were aggressively escorted off the bus one at a time and directed into the chapel. In the top far end corner of the doorway, I noticed a Holy Bible being used as a door stopper. I was taken aback.

A six-foot-three, two-hundred-and-fifty-poundish White man was dressed in bright orange prison body armor. He held a three-foot oak wood stick in one hand and lightheartedly patted the tip of this head-cracking weapon in the palm of the other. Observing my dis-covery, he sinfully smirked behind his face shield and said, "Welcome to hell."

I fake-laughed, mugged his bitch ass, and kept walking. I wasn't upset by his sarcastic little tough-man comment. I was raised in hell. I grew up on the Southside of Chicago in widely known hoods such as the Wild Hundreds, Terror Town, and Death Valley—need I say more?

Besides, I was used to the police talking shit. I was more upset by the blatant disrespect they displayed for the Word of God. Maybe that's the real reason why they call this place "The Pit."

An additional hour later, the last bus occupant exited the pen-itentiary Gray Goose and entered the chapel, and the shackles were finally removed from my feet, waist, and hands. Hallelujah! Next, we were placed in line to be strip-searched by Orange Crush. Just my fucking luck, I was placed in the line of Officer Tough-Ass-Comment.

A strip-search consists of three different phases. Part one: you have to get completely naked in front of a male correctional officer. Part two: while the same bopper carefully searches through your gear, you have to stand there like Adam in the garden of Eden before he partook in the Tree of Knowledge. After apparel inspection, if no contraband is found, every article of clothing is dropped on the dirty prison floor right next to the same C/O. And part three, which is the most dehumanizing of this trifecta, naked as a gay-bird you unwill-ingly comply while every nook, cranny, and sacred orifice of your body is scanned by the same copper.

The officer starts at the top of your head, and if you have a nog-gin full of hair, he harshly runs his gloved fingers through it. Then he looks inside your ears and behind them. Next, you have to say, "Aaaahhhhhhhhhhh!" big and wide, affording the shakedown officer a perfect view into your mouth, throat, and space under your tongue. Directly after, you have to place both index fingers inside the sides of your mouth regardless if your fingers are clean or not, so the po-po can check for drugs and weapons within the boundaries of your jaw.

Following, you have to lift both arms high in the air, as if you're being held at gunpoint during an armed robbery, so the C/O can examine your armpits for hidden contraband. Soon after, you have to raise up your frank and beans and move your genitals from right to left for God knows what.

Next, you have to turn around with your back facing the same correctional officer and bend over at the waist like an exotic dancer trying to pay her way through college. Then you are forced to grab your booty meat with both hands and open your asshole big and wide, so the twist can look deep inside your anus with a power-outage flashlight like a first-year proctologist. *Click.* Now hold that position and cough, to ensure that you aren't keistering any drugs or weapons within your sphincter muscles. *Click.* Last but not least, turn back around, spread your toes, one-eighty once again, and show the police the bottom of your feet.

If all is clear, you meekly pick up your clothing, 'cause ain't nobody hard after experiencing some disturbingly violent shit like that. Then like a Geisha, you move out the way for the next victim and silently get dressed.

I was next to the last man to be shaken down by Officer Tough-Ass. The first guy in line got humiliated and disrespected even more than what was routinely required during a strip-search.

He breezed through phases one and two with no problem. But after the most dehumanizing point of phase three (which is the opening up of your ass, if you haven't guessed by now), Officer Tough-Ass started with the bullshit.

"Turn around and do it again," Officer Tough-Ass sternly said.

"What?" the inmate responded.

"You heard me, do it again!" Officer Tough-Ass harshly yelled.

The man hesitantly complied. He turned back around, bent over once more, opened his asshole up, and coughed even harder than before. And when he turned back around, all you heard reverberating throughout the chapel was *"Do it again!"*

Round three, what little piece of dignity and self-respect this brother once held flew out the window like ten trapped tweety-birds in a four-foot house full of hungry alley cats.

With tears in his eyes, the brother complied once more.

"Now get your shit and sit over there!" Officer Tough-Ass instructed with malice. *"Next!"*

The White dude before me stood, avoided making eye contact with Officer Tough-Ass, and unwillingly stepped into the lion's den.

I ain't gonna lie, my first thought was *I bet you he don't do that shit to the White boy.* Phase one and two went off without a hitch. But when the man turned around from bussing his booty-hole open, Officer Tough-ass started again.

"Turn back around and do it again!" he violently shouted.

When I'm wrong, I'm wrong, and I'll be the first to admit it. I automatically assumed that Officer Tough-Ass was on some racist-ass Jim Crow bullshit. But after seeing what I saw, I stood corrected. This dirty bitch appeared to be an equal-opportunity asshole. He saw no color, which is a good thing. But at the same time the misuse of his correctional authority as a way of fulfilling some sick and twisted desires in the name of dominance and emasculation cancels that little good out.

Oh shit, I'm next, I thought in my head.

I don't know what I'm a do if this evil bitch asks me to open my ass up more than once. Because it's clear to me and every inmate around and maybe even a few C/O's that Officer Tough-Ass gets off on humiliating people and he's begging for a reason to use that oakwood stick.

Have you ever been hit with a riot stick before? Know that when wielded properly, or improperly for that matter, whatever that demonic-ass weapon smack up against is gonna bust or break. Believe that! I'm not a hard motherfucker, nor am I stupid. So I ain't trying to get my head busted or ribs cracked today, or any other day for that matter. I experienced enough of that shit in the Cook County Jail. But in the same breath, I definitely don't want to keep busting my ass open in front of everybody like a double-barrel shotgun.

"Fuck it!"

I decided right then and there to *stay hard*. It was too late to get scared now, because me and Officer Tough-Ass already had words out in front of the chapel.

"*Next!*" he yelled, as my crying White comrade grabbed his clothing and moved to the side.

So I mugged up and looked him straight in his motherfucking eyes and I did not avert my optic lenses for a single moment. Honestly, I don't even remember blinking during this penitentiary standoff, and being true to the moment, neither did Officer Tough-Ass.

"*Turn around and squat!*" he said with authority.

I waited about five hella-long seconds before I did my one-eighty, and after the booty deed was done, I slowly turned back around to resume our smart-eyeing game. And just when I thought Officer Tough-Ass was about to yell, "Do it again!" he said, "Now let me see your feet!"

Alhamdulillah! I pronounced in my mind.

"Now get your shit and sit down!" were Officer Tough-Ass's final words to me, and I complied with gangsterish haste.

Prison can make you paranoid if you consistently attempt to predict human behavior for survival. So I automatically assumed that Officer Tough-Ass had his fill of humiliating us when he made our White comrade cry in public.

I was wrong again; the last guy behind me had to buss down three extra times before he was allowed to get dressed.

Personal application analysis

I maintained eye contact with Officer Tough-Ass even though I was in an inferior position. Solid eye contact leveled the playing field by nonverbally reminding Mr. Tough-Ass that I'm a man just like him; we eat, sleep, shit, and bleed the same way (rule 5).

I acted like I was mad as fuck and held that facial expression for all the world to see (rule 4). Honestly, I wasn't angry at all. I was more pissed off over the fact that I would have had to open my ass up one hundred times if instructed to avoid an ambulance ride to an outside hospital or the city morgue. Fuck that, I'm trying to go home wearing street clothes, not a body bag.

All in all, the other three guys in my strip-search line got treated, and I was able to avoid stark maleficence by maintaining eye contact and acting mad. My system works; it really works.

RULE 6

Do Not Accept Commissary!

Do not—I repeat with the seriousness of a bomb-disarming special-ist—do not accept commissary, food, or snacks from anyone. I don't care if this person is one of your homeboys from the street or a blood relative, kindly refuse their offering.

The gratuitous ones may look the same, laugh the same, and talk the same, but their thoughts may not be the same. Remember, prison can change any good man in remarkably evil ways. That is just a fact that comes along with the pressures of incarceration. Now I know I may sound a little paranoid, speaking ill about your homie-homie or a blood relative. Trust me, I have heard of homeboys tearing off homeboys, uncles raping nephews, and fathers setting out sons, all in the name of dominance, pleasure, and faggotry. So beware, you've been warned.

Do I really need to tell you not to accept anything from a stranger? In the interest of safety, I guess I do, because common sense ain't so common these days.

Do not accept anything from a complete stranger? Why not? They're fucking strangers! You don't know them people. Granted, they may have good intentions and are shining representatives of the Golden Rule. Then again, it could all be a sham. I don't think you want to gamble your sweet little pink asshole or the warmness of your supple mouth on the reasons for such niceties inside a cold-blooded hypermasculine environment. Do you?

So to make sure that all bases are covered, here is a list of items you should never receive in any shape, form, or fashion while in prison: candy bars, hard candy, honey buns, cupcakes, cookies, Twinkies, meat products (dicks included), chips, chicken, fish, cereal, milks, and juices. In short, never accept merchandise from the inmate commissary, and that also includes hygiene items such as soap, deodorant, toothpaste, hair care products, tissue, write-outs, etcetera.

I advise that you do without, and patiently wait until a family member, loved one, or friend sends money to your inmate trust fund account. Then you can purchase all the items that you may need or want. In the meantime, in between time, every meal served in the county jail or state prison has been weighed and measured. So it holds just enough calories, nutrients, and protein for you to make it to the next scheduled meal. Three hots and a cot baby!

Now the food may taste like Eukanuba dog food warmed over but you will have a full belly after waiting the proper ten-to-fifteen-minute digestion period.

Equally, do not accept any two-for-ones, three-for-ones, or anything in that manner. Calmly wait for your outside money to hit your books. Two-for-one is prison's most popular version of the interest rate charges; worldly credit card users have to pay the moment that their card has been swiped.

For clarity, let's just say I run a two-for-one store, which means that all the products that the inmate commissary has, so do I. But instead of charging you singularly for each item like the canteen, I tax you double the amount for my goods. Only the strong survive, so yes, I am taking full advantage of your cravings, stupidity, and lack of self-restraint.

Moreover, in prison your word is like a credit card. So if you asked and received a pack of chocolate chip cookies from my store, when your money comes in you would repay me two packs of said cookies, two for one. Understand?

Prison credit 101 at its finest. The only difference between worldly credit and prison credit is that if you cannot pay your out-standing bill in the world, you can timely file for bankruptcy and be relatively safe. In prison, if you are unable to pay your tab, filing for bankruptcy is equivalent to being forced to hold knives and drugs, perform sexual acts, and/or become a human punching bag. No one should have to live like that. So please practice self-restraint and go without until your peoples can get at you.

Now, if you are unable to receive any dinero from the outside world to be placed on your books, all is not lost. Still adhere to rule 6 and don't accept shit from anyone. And here's how you move to receive the items you may need or want. Sell your sweet-tight ass and that long-moist throat for five dollars a pop and you won't ever want for nothing!

Naw, I'm just fucking with you. But you will have to sell or trade off the few good items that come to you free from your state trays. State trays at times include edible meals such as fried chicken, baked chicken, fish, hamburgers and fries, cakes, and cookies. Those institutional delicacies can be bartered for soap, deodorant, noodles, candy bars, and various other commissary items.

You are just going to have to lose a little weight to get the things you require to survive. No worries; we all can stand to drop a pound or two, right? Better that than getting your ass and face blew out from correctional sex or violence.

In all, for my big-pencil brothers who have not caught on by now, there is no such word as "free" in prison. Everything costs something. Even the food, clothing, shelter, and Medicare that your institution "freely" provides are costing you irreplaceable moments of your life.

Personal application of rule 6

After the strip search in Menard's chapel, we were all taken to the North Cell House, gallery 8 for intake, which is also called "receiving." Intake lasts thirty days. Throughout this period, all new inmates are processed and classified before being released into the general population or safely escorted to protective custody.

During intakes' grueling penitentiary gauntlet, you "receive" your bedding, clothing, personal property, and a full dental and medical overhaul. In addition, you are forced to have a little chat with mental health officials to determine if you are homicidal, suicidal, or in need of psych medication to level off any chemical imbalance within your brain. Also during this time, your disciplinary record, aggression level, and intake behavior will be scrutinized then weighed and measured. The end result of this administrative review will determine your housing unit.

My four-week stint in receiving was spent with a guy name Big Will. He was a six-foot-two, two-fifty-pound-over black country boy with hands the size of back catcher mitts. So I politely offered him the bottom bunk even though I was the first man to the cell. He happily accepted. There wasn't much room for walking around, let alone standing, in a five-by-seven-foot-wide, eight-foot-high living space outfitted with a bunk bed, two wooden thirteen-inch television stands, and a porcelain toilet and sink.

Back then, you weren't allowed to go to commissary while in receiving. That was a fucked-up rule considering we could only purchase two deodorants and two bars of soap at a time. I had about four bars of Ivory soap and two Dial roll-on deodorants in my stash, and Big Will was holding around the same.

Two weeks in, we both ran out of that little-ass roll-on deodorant. Now instead of using our soap just to shower with twice a week and hoe-bath with on the remaining days, we were forced to wash up at least three times a day and use the same soap as a pseudodeodorant to battle a musty-ass body odor that the down south September heat was extracting from our bodies. Now for those of us who have had to use soap in place of deodorant, know that it doesn't cover much, and if you move your arms around too often, it suds up and emits an exotic-musk smell.

Adhering to rule 6, me and my cellmate wouldn't accept shit from nobody. By week three, we both were fed up with our overused pantry space smelling like an enclosed training camp for gorillas in the mist. Big Will took action. He snuck a commissary slip in with the general population gallery beneath us.

I laughed to myself because I didn't think that shit would ever work. Wrong again. Two days later, around lunchtime, a goofy-ass officer busted down the cell door and yelled, "Williams, commissary!"

As Big Will got dressed, the bopper had a look on his face like our holistic ambiance smacked the shit out of his nose.

An hour later, Big Will came back with a big-ass bag of merch. Not only was I musty but I was hungrier than two drunk motherfuckers in a homeless shelter serving line.

"Rasheed, you want some of this food?" he offered with a smile

"Naw, I'm straight,"

"I know you hungry. You can put it back when you go to the store."

"I'm cool bro," I shot right back.

Man, he had everything: summer sausage, Doritos, candy bars, pops, Little Debbie cakes, etcetera. My mouth was watery as hell while he ate all types of goodies, but still I refused to violate rule 6.

"You want one of these deodorants?" he asked.

"I told you I'm straight, I don't need nothing."

"Man you ain't finta sit in here smelling like WrestleMania while I'm trying to eat. You better take this deodorant." And he threw it in my lap.

I laughed because his wordplay fit the occasion at hand. I've never been to a professional wrestling event but I'm sure this cell's aroma was quite similar to center stage at WrestleMania under those big, bright lights.

"We got baked chicken tonight," I said. "I know how you like that. You can have mine for this deodorant."

"Man I got enough food and I know you hungry, so keep your chicken and hit me back later."

"You either take that chicken tonight for this deodorant or it's gonna smell like a Royal Rumble in this bitch 'cause I'm finta start doing push-ups in the bed."

"All right man," he responded with a grin.

Day thirty, we were moved to the South Lowers. And even though Big Will was cool as fuck, I was informed, as soon as I hit population, that he had a sex crime. So I had to create some distance between us because that musty-ass situation would have been a bonding experience for any two men.

Getting out the way hurt a little bit, but it was easy at the same time because I ain't owe him shit. Baked chicken goes for a dollar in Menard and that little-ass deodorant costs sixty-nine cents. Where I'm from, fair exchange ain't never been a robbery.

Personal application analysis

In summary, by not accepting any commissary from Big Will and by paying for that deodorant with my baked chicken (rule 6), I was able to avoid befriending a sex offender. This new friendship would have inadvertently made me semisusceptible to a distinct type of penitentiary entanglement.

RULE 7

Do Not Gamble

Just as hypertension, heart disease, and diabetes are the leading causes of death among African Americans, in a similar manner gambling, gambling debts, and gambling-related instances are the principal designs for death amid Illinois prisoners.

Six out of every ten fights in the clink stems from a gambling-related incident in one way or another. So if you want to block a whole lot of violence-induced punches before they are ever thrown, do not bet on sporting events; refrain from sitting down at any card, chessboard, or domino tables; and flee with haste from every clickity-clack session.

Games of chance are a no-no in prison and should be avoided at all times. Even a small gentleman's bet could lead to a major unraveling of brutality and mayhem, so stay clear.

The real gamble in prison is whether or not your opponent will pay up if he loses. So the question is, what are you willing to do to get paid?

For example, let's just say you made a ten-dollar bet with Little Shit-Starter and your baseball team won. Then when you come to collect, Little Shit-Starter says, "Fuck you, I ain't paying you shit Now come get it like Tyson!"

What are you going to do? These little-ass cells aren't built for hand-to-hand combat. So if you run in there on him, y'all get to tussling, and he hit his head on something and dies—you ain't never going home. 'Cause a jailhouse murder will always equal a natural life sentence.

Same scenario; let's just flip the coin. You run off into his cell to take what's rightfully yours (ten dollars), and he kills you in the process. You're going home but in a way that is not beneficial to you. You feel me?

Final illustration. Little Shit-Starter just popped off at you, ending with, "Now come get it like Tyson!"

You decide to be the bigger man.

Fuck that. Ten dollars ain't worth fighting fo. I'm just not gonna gamble with him anymore.

Now that's fine and dandy in normal society, but you're in an abnormal prison setting, and word will travel around fast about how you let Little Shit-Starter punk you out your ten dollars. So from here on out you'll be viewed as "sweet."

Still wanting to gamble, this time around you bet Johnny Rage and lose, so you pay up ten whole dollars' worth of delicious commissary, because that's what honorable gamblers do, right? Well, you bet Johnny Rage again, but this time around your fortune has changed and your team is victorious. Now when you happily attempt to collect your winnings, Johnny Rage starts with the bullshit.

"You better get the fuck on before I beat your ass. I ain't paying you shit!"

What you gonna do? And this depressingly evil cycle will continue until you are willing to fight for what is yours.

Violence is the only universal language in prison; it crosses color lines and breaks down all communication barriers.

Metaphorically speaking, gambling in jail is equivalent to wrapping some rusty-ass bob wire around your entire dick and balls and tying the other end of that wire to a speeding F-250 truck. *Ouch* ain't the motherfucking word, 'cause you finta bleed out in the worst way.

So stay the fuck away from gambling if you want to hold on to what matters the most. Life or death, the choice is easy for me. I'll promptly choose life every time and that nine-second tingly feeling that comes along with living a hedonistic life outside these prison walls. What about you?

Personal application of rule 7

I have never gambled during my entire bid. That was largely due to a stabbing incident I witnessed inside Cook County Jail. This man got stuck seven times over some state Kool-Aid. And the sounds he made while begging for mercy still haunts me till this very day. I told myself right then and there, "If a nigga will butcher you over some free Kool-Aid, imagine what someone might do to you for a few items of commissary." With such keen survivalist rationality, I said, "Fuck gambling," and chose life instead.

I reverted to Al-Islam in April of 1997. I was never much of a gangbanger, so I figured the transition would be easy, considering I didn't have too many enemies. After going through the proper channels, I turned around and started walking toward Allah.

I have never missed a commissary day, thanks to my moms, family, and childhood friends, Alhamdulillah. So my property box stayed decent, and I always came back from the store holding a nice-sized bag filled with all my favorite comfort foods. I am not bragging right now; I'm just trying to make a point.

One day, after returning from commissary with big bags, a nigga came to my door talking about, "Shorty G say you got them two bricks of squares?"

"Two bricks for what? He can't be talking about me 'cause I don't owe him nothing."

His errand boy left and came back a few minutes later.

"He say you owe him two bricks for that Bulls-Pacers game."

"I don't even gamble, so I know he trippin'."

"I didn't think you did," the errand boy said as he walked back to Shorty G's cell.

"Sheed, what you wanna do?" Nazim, my Muslim brother and childhood friend since the seventh grade, announced as I turned back from the bars.

"Calm down brah, dude ain't on nothing."

"He call his self trying to extort you 'cause you ain't hooked up no more."

Nazim took those words right out of my head. But I concealed my anger because I needed to handle this little situation on my own. Plus my homie got a tendency, since we were young, of going too far.

I wasn't trying to stay locked up for the rest of my life. So I decided to just break his jaw when the doors rolled for being disrespectful. The rules we lived by warranted that action. And such a defiant stand would visually scream to the prison population that I have never needed a mob standing behind me to be a man.

The errand boy returned.

"Rasheed, I hollered at him for you. I told him that I ain't never seen you gambling, you ain't never even played a parley ticket, so he must have you confused with someone else."

"What he say then?" I respond.

"That I was right. He had you mixed up with Lil Trav."

"All right."

"Okay" were the last words he said before moving on.

Personal application analysis

Shorty G was attempting to extort me in a roundabout way because me and Lil Trav looked nothing alike. He was light-skinned, tall, and skinny with a fat-ass Redd Foxx stomach. I'm short, stocky, and caramel-complected with boyishly good looks. I guess Shorty G figured that I needed to pay punk fees since I no longer represented a flag.

Once again, I have never gambled while in prison (rule 6). So my reputation preceded me, and it was a loud voice inside a circle that I could never have reached without being violent.

Added bonus of gilla

Staying true to my journalist integrity, I have to say there are some benefits to gambling. Like when you make a bet, win, and get paid. But the bad that comes along with games of chance far outweighs the good.

Gambling keeps you from the remembrance of God (if you believe in that sort of thing). Gambling also twists your mind to the degree that wrong becomes fair-seeming. And if you continue down that winding road, you could end up morally bankrupted, like this guy here who I used to carry as a brother and friend.

Back in 1996, I held one of the better institutional jobs at Joliet Correctional Center, a maximum-security prison in Joliet, Illinois. I worked for the front side of the industries. There we produced mattresses and pillows for every detention camp, reformatory, and penitentiary in the state. My homeboy worked on the other side of the industries, where he was gainfully employed as a data entry operator.

One morning on the way to work, a conversation exposed just how far his gambling addiction had thrown him over the ethical edge of probity.

"Dog what's up?" I asked him.

"Shit man, just pissed off. I lost that little money yesterday."

"Yeah."

"It wasn't nothing but two bricks, but still."

"What you bet on?"

"I sat down at that poker table in the gym."

"Man you lucky you only got hit for forty bucks. It be hundreds and thousands of dollars circulating around that shady-ass table. What else going on?"

"I called my mom the other night and told her she needed to wire me one hundred dollars before they kill me."

I wasn't able to make the connection at that time with the gambling debt. All I heard was, *Somebody wanna kill him!*

Back then, if someone threatened your life, it wasn't an idle rambling of words. It was more like a murderous vow to be fulfilled with haste.

"Who the fuck you talking about?" I responded, ready to transform into battle mode.

"Naw we cool. I just told my mama that shit over the phone so she would hurry up and run that money."

"That's what's up," I calmly put forth.

But my thoughts were in direct contradiction to those words. I was thinking.

How in the fuck could he do such a thing to the woman who cared for him and nurtured him?

What if she went without lunch at her place of employment or groceries for the whole week?

What if she wasn't able to pay her rent and got evicted that month?

What if she injured herself or even died in a car accident as she raced to the currency exchange to wire him that little money?

This nigga ain't my brother or friend. He can't give a fuck about me if he would violate his mother's love and trust in such an insidiously evil way. And I'd be a damn fool to put my life on the line or even go back-to-back with a dirty nigga like that.

The killer part about this whole situation is that he didn't have to pay them guys at the poker table shit. They would have held them two bricks over his head, barring him from the table, just to keep him out the way. Because they were hustling for real, from count-check to count-check, making big money.

In brief, gambling is a doorway that leads to many other doors of evil. Like I said before, your mind can become twisted to the point where wrong becomes fair-seeming. And you'll end up abusing and mistreating the very people who love you the most. Learn from Dogs' story and abstain from gambling while in prison before you lose your mind.

RULE 8

Fight! Fight! FIGHT!

I've been fighting my whole life in one way or another. And whether you realize this or not, so have you. The mere fact of you reading these words is testimony to that truth. Out of millions and millions of sperms cells, you swam the hardest and the fastest to fertilize that egg. You were fighting before you even knew or understood the word.

This innate disposition for combat has already been placed inside you. Thank God, Yahweh, Jehovah, Jesus, evolution, or whoever. But know you are genetically designed to battle. So why not tap into this war pool of assertive resistance? 'Cause you're gonna need it where you're going.

Fighting is a violent interpersonal exchange, and as sure as a girl's fart stink, you will have to tussle with someone in prison; it is just a matter of time. For the nonbelievers, what else do you think transpires in a hypermasculine environment filled to capacity with an overabundance of angry, violent, misled, dysfunctional, fully grown boys masquerading as men? Basket weaving? Fuck no! We fight, *fight,* FIGHT!

Hand-to-hand combat is the only activity in prison where you can flat-out lose but still win. Sounds crazy, right? Well, let me see if I can make it plain. Mano a mano, if you get to brawling and win, you'll be accepted. On the other hand, if you get your ass handed to you on a silver platter and avoid involving the authorities, not only will you be accepted but respected. Why? Well, for one, everyone around hates the police. And two, anyone who has ever been on the losing end of a fisticuff knows that a good ass-whoopin' builds character, so welcome to manhood.

Personal application of rule 8

Case in point, I'm a share with you my worst loss because it applies to the subject at hand, and in the end, it turned out to be my greatest victory.

So y'all don't get it twisted, for the record I'm 86–6 with one draw inside the Department of Corrections. Yeah, I know, that's a lot of goddamn fights. And out of those six losses, I only cried out to Allah one time for help.

The draw? Now, I know a lot of guys say that a fight is a tie to cover up the fact that they got they ass beat. But this ain't that. Some scary-ass nigga called me a bitch one time then ran, and I've been looking for his ass ever since. That's why I say I got a draw. Because he had enough heart to call me a bitch! *Me!* But he broke out so fast that Usain Bolt couldn't generate enough speed to catch up with him to continue our conversation. He did that!

I digress. I can't remember the exact year this fight took place. Yeah, that ass-whoopin' was just that traumatic. But I was in Menard

Correctional Center at that time working the 1:00 p.m.–6:00 p.m. shift in the inmate kitchen as a food server.

Carceral fact: It is an unwritten rule for you to draw close to the individuals who wear their hats the same way that you do.

Me, being the type of man who has always thought outside the box while trapped within, befriended a guy from the other side. Toot and I got cooler than two oscillating fans plugged into the same extension cord inside an air-conditioned room.

We lived a cell apart on gallery 8 in the South Uppers. It was commissary day, so I went with the first half of shoppers, and Toot shot off with the second group.

When he came back, I noticed he had about four bags of Jay's Hot Stuff potato chips, and I wanted some.

"Toot, let me hold a bag of them chips until next week."

"Which ones?"

"The Hot Stuff man. They ain't have them joints when I went."

"I'm finta throw 'em."

"Slow down cuzo, we come out for work in like twenty minutes."

"Man you better take these chips."

He threw the bag, and it landed in front of my cell on the dirty concrete floor.

Word to Buddha, I didn't care that he threw them chips on the ground. I've eaten off the prison floor before. I was pissed over the fact that he tossed my food to me like a dog who was begging.

Yeah, I know, that sounds stupid even as I write it. Have mercy, 'cause my mentality was real fucked up back then.

"Why you throw them chips?"

"I'm trying to get my shit together before we leave for work."

"I'm leaving them chips right there until you hand 'em to me."

"What if the police come man?"

"Well, one gone, and I ain't putting 'em back neither. 'Cause I told you not to throw 'em."

Real talk: at this point, I was just joking, spitting my usual level of bullshit. Because if I stuck my mirror through the bars and saw a bopper coming our way, I would have made them chips disappear from the gallery like David Blaine. In my mind, it has always been us against them and ain't no changing that.

"Sheed, you better pick them chips up before I beat your little ass."

I laughed.

"You ain't gonna do shit to me. Fuck you and them chips."

"Man why you on this pussy-ass shit!" Toot yelled from the back of his cell.

Quick side note: Behind the wall, the words *pussy* and *bitch* are fighting words; no ifs, ands, or buts about it.

"What you say?" I shot back, hoping I didn't hear what I just heard.

"Nigga you heard me. I'm tired of this pussy-ass shit you be on!"

Yep, I heard right. So I jumped straight into verbal judo mode.

"Naw nigga, you be on some pussy-ass shit around here!" I screamed with malice.

"All right, I'm a see if you say that shit at work!"

"Man I'll say it to your mama!"

Following that statement there was a deafening silence, and just that fast, another penitentiary fight was scheduled.

For years, Toot and I lightheartedly talked shit back and forth for fun. During that time I have never seen him lose his cool, and our verbal frolicking never veered off into the traffic lane of physical violence.

After all the laughs we shared, I had to give him the benefit of the doubt. I figured he blew his top because he got some unwanted news from home or maybe he was just having a bad day. In spite of the backlash I was sure to receive from my carceral peers, if Toot had apologized for dropping a "word bomb," I would have shook his hand like a man, and we could've kept it pushing like the incident was all a bad scene from a Hollywood casting couch.

The officer busted down the doors for work, and we belled into the kitchen to perform our respective duties.

Every food server had to make two racks of cups and place inside each cup a spork with one salt and pepper pack. Our line supervisor Ms. Butterface ordered me to go with her to the vegetable house for the daily serving of juices and milks. I grabbed a rolling cart and we followed close behind. Once inside, I snatched up fifty crates full of four-ounce apple juices and ten crates full of six-ounce cartons of skim milk, stacking them five crates high onto the loading cart.

Pulling such a heavy load all by myself was extremely difficult. But I kept a cool demeanor like I wasn't straining 'cause after all, there was a lady present. Communication is 80 to 85 percent non-verbal, so when Ms. Butterface smiled my way, I could tell that she knew this cart full of juices and milks was fucking me up. But instead of asking for assistance, I smiled back as if I had it all under control. Sexism in America runs deep; even men in prison are affected by this societal ill.

I'm sure if I'd asked Ms. Butterface to help me out, she would have given me a hand. I had been oriented after years of conditioning to act in a certain manner whenever a lady was present. Mentally at that time, I was not strong enough to fight back against all that male chauvinist patriarchal bullshit. Added to this, if the homies saw her helping me, they would have never let me live that one down. Joke after joke was sure to be told about how weak I was for needing a "lady's help." Shitted, I probably would have had to scrape like ten more niggas behind that, knocking me up to 96–6–1.

Anyway, I evenly distributed all the milks and juices among the four serving line coolers. I rolled the cart back up to the front, walked to the back of the kitchen, and dipped into the restroom to take a Bohemian piss. Halfway through my urination, I heard someone step inside the bathroom. Looking over my shoulder, I saw Toot stretch his arms high in the air as if he's getting ready for a fight. I cut my urination short, turned around, and quickly went into a 402 Conference. I'm five foot eight—five foot nine on a tall day—and I weighed about one sixty with rocks in my pocket, in the rain, holding a diabetic baby. Toot stood about six foot two and weighed two twenty with about 19 percent body fat. I really didn't wanna mix it up with this country-fed motherfucker, and for the record that don't make me scary; it means I'm smart.

"Toot, you serious? You wanna fight me over some chips you gave me?"

"I'm just tired of your mouth. You always talking shit."

"Man, I said you on some pussy-ass shit in defense after you said it to me first."

After that sentence, I scanned Toot's body and observed him standing on his pivot foot. I knew right then and there that our conversation had ended. So I stole first, throwing a jab, which was immediately followed by a right hand—BAM! BAM!—but I ain't knock his ass out.

His head landed on my shoulder, and he wrapped his arms around my body as I struggled to get free. Seconds turned into minutes as he recovered from my initial assault. When Toot finally released me, he pushed me off him, creating distance between us.

I threw another right hand and felt his lead hand strategically guide my punch over and down toward the floor, then *bam!* I felt the vengeful wrath of his right hand, which caused me to see a burning-bright light and hear that annoying public service announcement beep simultaneously.

My knees buckled, and I felt myself going down. *Bam!* I couldn't tell you what punch that was. All I know is that it woke me out of my flash-bang stupor. I swung wildly with my left hand. He blocked it by moving his right hand up and over to his ear like some shit you see on TV. Then he popped off like five jabs to my face with lightning speed and accuracy—*pop, pop, pop, pop,* and *pop.*

In retaliation, I threw a lazy right hand; he slipped my punch, then busted my nose. BAM! Blood splattered everywhere, and my eyes instantly sweat. I grabbed hold of him, attempting to wrestle him down, because I couldn't do shit with his hands. Still punch drunk, he scooped me in no time at all and slammed me to the hard floor, BA-BOOM!

I wound up by a crate with a plastic bag in it filled with industrial bleach. I gripped the corners and was in the process of slinging it over my head in an attempt to blind him. But Toot peeped game, slid right behind me on his knees, locked his arm around my neck, cutting off my air, and trapped me in the sleeper-hold.

"Let go of my neck," I squealed in my Gilbert Godfrey voice.

"Let go of the bleach," Toot responded like James Earl Jones.

I promptly complied because I wasn't trying to get choked out in prison; you could wake up a different kind of man.

We stood back up and squared off once again. Every punch I threw, beating the shit out the air, he landed about five or six Mike Tyson blows to my face and head. And his arsenal of pugilistic combinations was coming from all different angles. With not much gas left in my tank, "AAAAAAAHHHHHHHH!" I screamed loud as hell and rushed him with my head down like a raging bull. He stepped to his right and caught me in my neck with a fierce-ass uppercut. "Uuummppp!" was the sound extracted from my esophagus.

Head up and swinging wildly now with both hands, I lightly grazed his chin. What the fuck did I do that stupid-ass shit for? Because he took me to a whole new level of ass-kickery.

No bullshit, I was trapped in the corner with my back against the wall, and he threw a thirty-seven punch combination, and all of them landed. How could I have known the exact number of strikes? Well, I simply counted the number of times that the back of my head bounced off the cemented wall.

When I got to number twenty-seven, I realized that Toot had no intentions of stopping. Being powerless to put an end to such a magnificent ass-whoopin', I cried out to the Creator of the heavens and earth, sincerely screaming in my head, "Oh Allah, *please* get this nigga off me, 'cause he trying to kill me!"

And in that instant, my prayer was answered. One of the guys who was in a position of power for his team stepped into the bathroom and said, "Toot that's enough. It's over with."

And as calm as ever, Toot stopped punching me and backed away. For you atheists, I'm here to tell you God is real.

Anyway, a Christian brother came into the bathroom with three clean T-shirts. He threw Toot one and came my way with the other two. Venting, I yelled in Toot's direction, "Man from here on out you do your time, and I'm a do my time, and we goin' keep it like that!"

Toot ignored my comment because he did all his talking with his hands. Then he snatched off his T-shirt that was soaked in my blood, dropped it in the crate with bleach, rinsed his hands and face, and walked out wearing a brand-new T like ain't nothing happened.

"I know bro, calm down," said the representative of Jesus.

He slowly pulled my bloody shirt off my body and dropped it into the crate while I rinsed my face in the sink. Then he wrapped the first T-shirt around my entire head, and I held it there to stop the bleeding as he guided my head and arms through the holes of the second T.

I don't know if it was my adrenaline or the shock from that ass-whoopin' but I honestly didn't think it was that bad until Big Fred came charging in as I dropped the final bloody shirt inside the crate.

"What the fuck happened?" he roared.

"I just had a fight."

"Did they jump you?"

"Naw nigga, it was one-on-one."

"You wanna tear this bitch up?"

I could've called a play but wisely decided against that move. Why? A lot of people would have seriously got hurt. And once an internal investigation was done, the truth would have revealed that I didn't take my ass-kicking like a man and I put all my homeboys' lives on the line over a bag of Jay's Hot Stuff potato chips. Unlucky me surely would have been put in violation and beat only half to death.

Personal application analysis

A couple months passed, and I would still hear a joke or two about how swoll my head got. Toot hurt me bad and lowered my self-esteem. But the overall consensus of the environment gave me the strength to hold my head up high. Because I took my beating like a man and I didn't involve the authorities in our affairs (rule 8).

In conclusion, if you're pushed, slap, spit on, punched, treated, or verbally challenged with carceral no-no words—fight! *fight!* FIGHT! And you'll be accepted and respected, and your time spent in prison will go a whole lot smoother. Trust and believe.

Added bonus of gilla

Now I know I'm a lose a whole lot of kool-points when I say this, but fuck kool-points, it's all about survival right now. If it's more than one person trying to fight you, or you have that innate feeling that the scuffle may start out one-on-one but ultimately end with you being jumped and you ain't got any homeboys, RUN! And get help from the police. Always remember, those who run away live to fight another day, and ain't no shame in that.

RULE 9

Beware Booty Bandits

When I first entered the prison system, booty banditism was at an all-time high. You had convicts in positions of power using their authority to literally take advantage of the new booties to the system. You had aggressive-ass rape-a-men who lifted weights twice a day and three times on Sundays, using their muscles and strength to strong-arm that ass-play. Then you had the mentally predatorial homosexuals who used their "beautiful minds" to manipulate or trick intellectually weaker men out of that Hershey highway.

Yeah, there was a gang of unwanted ass-fucking and throat-stretching going on. Nowadays, thanks to an overhaul of security measures put in play by the Illinois Department of Corrections and the slow-but-steady acceptance within the minds of Americans in regard to homosexual activities, most booty bandits are unemployed and searching for correctional sex in nonviolent ways. But be alarmed, out of my mouth to your virgin ears, *you are not safe.* Booty bandits are still lurking. These evil-ass predatory creeps just haven't been given the right set of circumstances to practice their creepdom, so beware.

Have you ever heard the old adage that says, "It is better to be viewed as a man of intellect than to open your mouth and remove all doubt"?

Well, I got a jailhouse version: "It is wiser to be looked upon as someone who can handle himself than to horseplay with your incarcerated peers and remove all doubt."

Play fighting is one of the many tricks used by undercover rape-a-men as a means of testing your strength, fighting skills, and willpower, so don't do it.

Furthermore, avoid play wrestling at all costs because these homo-freaks will eagerly use this macho fun-loving activity as an avenue to grind and feel all over your body, sick motherfuckers!

Now I know that wearing the back of your pants right up under your booty meat is the style today and a way to stay on fleek. But in prison all sagging leads to are unwanted homosexual advances.

Check this. Imagine Kim Kardashian walking past you sagging a pair of creased-up, dark-blue khakis. You can clearly see her pretty little white panties. And all that juicy-as-booty meat is just hanging out and shaking for the entire world to see. Uuummm-humm-good.

Flip that. When you sag your pants in prison, inside the sick mind of a booty bandit, you're the male version of Kim Kardashian. Hey, Bruce Jenner!

Now for those of you who still don't understand what I am trying to say, let me see if I can be even more direct. If a straight man in prison chokes his chicken to visions of a female employee or some beautiful vixen inside a girly magazine, then what do you think a booty bandit pleasures himself to late at night? The same thing? Fuck no! He's masturbating to you and your exposed ass. So pull your pants up nigga, if you don't want another man jagging his dick late at night to mental pictures of your derriere.

Added bonus of gilla

When it is shower time, never turn your back to anyone, especially while washing your body. Equally at no time should you ever soap up your face and head. The safety of your asshole weighs heavily upon you being able to see. So always cleanse everything above your neck inside the secure space of your cell.

Moreover, never under any condition should you directly stare at the naked men around you. Relax and utilize your peripheral vision to patrol the bathing environment. Otherwise, you'll end up being labeled a dick watcher and bring down to your doorstep a Pandora's box full of unwanted bullshit.

Last but not least, and most importantly, don't drop the soap nigga! (Smile.)

RULE 10

Remember Self-Preservation

Please don't let my penitentiary jargon fool you. I am a man of character, and this rule here is the most difficult to write. I am about to advise you of something that once upon a time in my life, as a weaker man, I practiced wholeheartedly without fail. And it pains me to propagate such an inhumane lifestyle. But it has to be done in the interest of *you* returning home safely.

There will be physically disabled men, elderly gentlemen, and mentally ill dudes doing time right next to you. These individuals will be laughed at, ridiculed, bullied, and mistreated in the worst ways. No matter how bad you may want to stop the abuse of those defenseless creatures of humanity, you can't and you shouldn't.

The law of self-preservation is the order every day and all night inside the pokey. This law needs to be utilized more efficiently than a toddler chasing behind an uncaring parent inside a crowded Walmart on Black Friday.

You may observe a mentally ill patient duped into drinking a cup of urine or toilet water. Now as off-putting as that may sound, this is the least amount of trauma that this chemically imbalanced man will endure. You can thank the stealing and gross negligence of our taxpaying dollars by the "powers that be" to the closing of most psychiatric facilities in Illinois.

Remember the filthy bum that you so easily drove by on the street? Perhaps he was heavily engaged in a heated debate with himself, pushing a shopping cart full of fecal matter clothing, and used Tupperware while wearing a neatly folded tinfoil hat in zero-degree weather? Yeah, that guy is being housed with violent and morally bankrupt man-wolves instead of receiving the kind and compassionate care that he so greatly deserves as an American, a human being, and creation of God. Somebody help us.

You may also witness a handicapped or hearing/visually impaired man being mocked without fail, physically abused, or sexually assaulted. Stand down! And mind your motherfucking business.

You may even see an elderly gentleman get his food taken by a younger, stronger, coward-ass predator. Stand down! That ain't your motherfucking granddaddy. Rule one that bitch and go home to the people who need you the most.

"Better him than me, that's how a nigga see" was one of my favorite mantras during my days of ignorance. Whenever I would see something mean, unjust, or so diabolically evil that it would bring tears to my eyes, I'd silently say, *Better him than me, that's how a nigga see.* And more times than not, the pain of adhering to the law of self-preservation would subside.

My personally prescribed mantra was similar to the dehumanizing names given to the Vietcong during the Vietnam War by American Soldiers: "gooks," "slope-heads," etcetera, were labels used to aid in perpetuating government-sanctioned acts of violence. But in all actuality, the Vietnamese were just regular old people like you and me fighting for their own way of life.

I'm not trying to justify my inaction or the ignorant creation of a penitentiary mantra to stay on the road to freedom. I'm just trying to make a point, which is that sometimes in life and even more so in prison, you will have to do some things that goes totally against your constitution in order to survive.

So *stand down!* Unless you are a made man or someone who is willing to put his freedom and life on the line for a complete stranger.

Personal application of rules 9 and 10

In 2002, I was twenty-six years old, trapped in "The Pit" and living in the South Lowers. This was one of the few occasions where I actually felt at ease behind the wall. My semicomfort was largely due to the fact that I was surrounded by a band of no-nonsense brothers. And every now and then, they looked toward me for guidance.

All my life, I've been regarded as a smart dude or someone who "knew the way." But honestly, I'm not that smart and I never knew the way. I'm just intense with common sense and have a good understanding of people.

Two doors down from my hut, an old-ass, late-sixties, six-foot-one, elderly-built, vocally impaired Black man moved into the cell with a skinny, five-ninish, early-forties cat from the hood. The handicapable chap had to place a battery-operated Passy Muir speaking valve against his voice box to speak. The dialect that sprung forth put you in the mind of a thugged-out R2-D2. You could clearly hear his robotic words echo throughout the cell house.

I can't even begin to tell you how many months passed before this incident occurred, because in prison, outside of violence, one day is identical to the next. Irregardless, one Saturday night around 1:30 a.m., I hear a loud-ass *smack!* Then the rumbling sounds similar to someone in Pamplona, Spain, running with the bulls.

A few minutes or so passed before all the ruckus stopped. Then you immediately hear the vocally impaired dude begging for mercy at the highest volume that his robotic electra-larynx could go:

"Please, man...! Stop...! I'm sorry! No! Don't...k-k-k-ill me— man! Nooooooo! Help! Pa-pa-pleeaase!"

By the way he paused in between his words and the faint smell of rusty pennies in the air, I knew he was being stabbed.

"N-n-n-noo! Pl-pleee! Sttooppp! You k-killing ma-ma-meee!"

On and on he went for about three distressing minutes straight, until an officer came around for his quarterly well-being check. This was the first time in my life that I was sincerely glad to see the police. And as soon as the bopper's shadow landed at the front of my door, one of the knife-wielder's comrades yelled out, "You bitch-ass officer, bring your punk ass here!"

And just like that, the unknowing officer ran straight past a crime scene in defense of his bruised ego.

"Where my money vouchers at?" the attention-grabber bark with fury.

"First off, I am not your bitch. Do I look like your mother? Second, I am not bringing you shit. And third, you better pipe down before I take your ass to segregation!" he responded with authority.

"I'm just fucking with you man. If you remember, can you bring me a money voucher when you come back this way? I'm trying to mail this shit out tomorrow."

"Watch your tone from here on out, and let me see what I can do."

And the officer left the gallery in the opposite direction from which he came. *Ca-clink!*

Once the back door locked, Mr. Knife went back to stabbing away.

"Ga-ga-God he-he-he-hel-hel-help, I'm sor-ry! I-I-I'm sor-sor-ry!"

I turned to my homeboy and said, "You think the old man gonna be able to last another fifteen minutes?"

"Naw, he dead."

"If that officer come back with that voucher, I'm a send him straight to that cell."

"Man you already know whatever you decide I'm riding with you."

So I sat back down and listened to this old man plead for his life with tears in my eyes. A couple more agonizing minutes passed, and the vocally impaired brother's battery began to wear out.

"Some———! Hell———Eeee! P-P-Ple———se!"

Ca-clink! I heard the front door open again. Sitting, I stuck my mirror through the bars and saw the po-po coming my way with a money voucher in hand. As soon as I stood up at the cell bars, the attention-grabber started calling the officer all types of bitches and hoes at the top of his lungs.

I decided right then and there to mind my motherfucking business. As much as I wanted to help the old dude, I wasn't willing to put neither my life nor the lives of my homies on the line for a man I didn't even know. So I sat back down.

As Officer Money Voucher picked up speed to confront the belligerent convict, he rightly noticed the pool of sanguine fluid that was forming outside the combatant's cell.

"Ten-ten, officer needs assistance!" the bopper yelled into his walkie-talkie as he inadvertently slipped into the puddle of blood.

Moments later, backup arrived, and Norman Bates's cousin calmly dropped his knife after one direct order, moved away from his victim, turned around, got cuffed up, and was taken to seg. Around this time, the nurses appeared and began to diligently work on the victim as he was hoisted away to the health care unit.

That night, I couldn't sleep a wink. I just knew the old man was dead. And the most unsettling part of it all was that I had the power to save him but stood down.

Better him than me, that's how a nigga see was all I kept repeating in my mind until we rolled out for lunch the next day.

The topic of all conversation was the stabbing incident. Word on the compound was that the old man got hit over thirty times and he still ain't die; talk about hard to kill. I was so relieved, better yet, elated, to hear that he had survived.

Now I want you to take a few moments and surmise why you think they got to tussling in the first place. Strike that—you'll never guess right, so let me just inform you of what the beef was all about.

This disabled old man had reached his hands into the piss-slot of his sleeping cellmate's boxer shorts and attempted to suck his *whole dick*. For real, I can't make this shit up. And I'd come to find out, orally raping hard sleepers had been his modus operandi for the past twenty years.

Check out the psychology and intent of this predatory dick sucker. He was hoping that under the guise of a wet dream/REM sleep, his victim would soundly sleep through the entire mouth-raping event. And if by chance his unsuspecting prey were to awaken, this super-creep hoped that his homosexual assault would magically turn into a "Dear Gay Penthouse" letter.

More times than not, his sick and depraved urges got him a well-whooped ass, which it appeared that the old man was willing to endure time and time again to receive that milky jackpot. Prison sucks, literally.

Personal application analysis

By adhering to the law of self-preservation (rule 10) I was able to avoid starting a war over a homosexual predator (rule 9). Such a military blunder would have inadvertently landed my body on the pointy end of a piece of Conan metal.

Carceral fact: We make fun of violence not just as a way to appear hard in a hypermasculine environment but also as a means of dealing with the trauma and pain of incarceration. So for the next week or so, we downplayed the justifiable butchering and cracked-penis related jokes about how his throat box got broke in the first place. True story.

RULE 11

Make Penitentiary Friends

Whether they are called friends of circumstance, friends of convenience, commissary friends, prison pals, or phony homies, there is strength in numbers, and you will need a friend to watch your back just as much as he'll need you. And once again, fair exchange ain't never been a robbery.

Now, I am not asking you to become a penitentiary politician and attempt to buddy up to everybody in the pod. Actions like that would be dangerous and stupid, and this book here is in direct opposition of those words. So however you decide to spend your time inside the big house, use that as an opportunity to make friends.

For example, since you are in the rare position of having a lot of free time on your hands, you may decide to work on your beach body while being boxed in. You can humbly ask to join a crew that's serious about fitness and build some needed camaraderie. Or you can pick out a like-minded individual at the same fitness level as yourself, exercise together, and build a bond that way.

Baseball, basketball, handball, soccer, or any available sporting activity—hell, even talking about sports can be used as a bridge to familiarity and friendship.

Card games, chess, and dominoes can be contentious hobbies in prison. So if you play only in the interest of having a little fun while passing time, not only will you pick up a few buddies along the way but you will be able to analyze your opponents' character and choose to circle your horses with the most congruous guys. Think of this as a penitentiary dating game minus the sex (smile).

Sharing a life skill is another way to gain some support from your surrounding area. For instance, if you can draw, or know anything about plumbing, electricity, heating, and air-conditioning repair, or fixing cars—*teach!* And you'll be respected, looked after, and treated with care.

A recent statistical survey in 2017 showed that 37 percent of all the inmates inside the Illinois Department of Corrections read below a sixth grade level. That truth is scary on so many different levels, because 97 percent of all convicted felons will be released back into society at some point in time. So if you can read, write, or think critically, teach the less fortunate and make lifetime friends while shaping the outside world into a better place.

If you have money, there will be a multitude of men around you who are dead broke. Do some good with your wealth and build alliances while making penitentiary friends. Here's how. Once or twice a week, make extra food and give it away to the poor, downtrodden, and hungry. Trust me, you'll see the ones who really need help, and if those souls are not visually accessible, just follow your heart.

Moreover, some of the men you offer sustenance may refuse your kind gesture. Do not take offence. They may be leery of your motives (rule 9) and/or staunch supporters of rule 6. Just be consistent with your alms to the poor, and your charitable acts will be seen by all for the good it provides.

Added bonus of gilla

While participating in sporting events or brain games, it is okay to crack a little lighthearted humor back and forth. But you never know the next man's trigger words, so be very mindful of your witty retorts while jesting, because verbal puns can quickly turn violent.

Personal application of rule 11

Around 1999ish in Menard Correctional Center, I was fortunate enough to receive a job in the inmate commissary. It was one of the best jobs I have ever had while incarcerated. From 7:30 a.m. till 2:30 p.m., I ate and drank to my stomach's desires. I'm talking Zero candy bars, heated honey buns, microwaved summer sausage and noodles, bottled water, delicious pops, chips—I had access to the whole shebang. As long as I did my job without complaint and marked off everything I smashed on the inventory sheet as damaged goods, my supervisors didn't care, and I happily chomped away.

The inside of the commissary was about the size of a three-lane bowling alley with connecting storage space fit for a small-town supermarket. All the products were protected by a floor-to-ceiling grammar school gate and three-inch pseudo-bulletproof Plexiglas. Firmly fixed behind those obstructions, you had a wooden, waist-high, two-foot-wide assembly line counter that ran from the front of the store all the way to the bagging windows.

There were six individual serving sections marked off by little holes drilled into the Plexiglas for talking points. We had little room to stand before the display shelves that stocked all the products the canteen had to offer.

The first space consisted of a variety of noodles, pops, and two-by-two-by-four-foot royal-blue plastic containers that were used to hold the inmates' commissary. The primary worker would position a tub on the assembly line counter, ask how many sodas and/or soups a customer wants, place those items within, and then slide the basket to me.

Beans and rice, cheese cups, coffee, mackerel, summer sausage, and tunas were the things you could grab from my spot. The next section contained various candy bars and hard candies. The following two areas comprised of hygiene products and an adjoining cabinet filled with cigarettes, cigars, and chewing tobacco. And the last shelves held all the chips, cookies, and Little Debbie cakes. Beyond that point were four strategically spaced computerized scanners and registers with two-by-two-foot latched windows for inmates to receive purchased items.

I never got tired of restocking my shelves or loading up those blue tubs with food because all the Tootsie Rolls and shit I was eating throughout the day kept me energized like a motherfucker.

Now I'm not calling nobody out or naming names (it is what it is). But a few of my coworkers refused to add items to customers' (fellow inmates') bins once they would pass their station. I never had a problem with going to retrieve anything, for anyone, from any section of the store. Because I knew what it felt like to forget to purchase something you should have ordered, go on lockdown for thirty days, then be sitting there looking hungry and stupid.

I also knew what it felt like to get to that computer, find out you have more money to spend, but no one wants to go back and load up your basket. So whenever a fellow convict forgot an item or had more lootchie than he thought, I'd move with haste to grab whatever was needed.

A year or so later, right after those planes brought down the Twin Towers on 9/11, I was fired from the commissary. Yeah, it was an attack on all Muslims, even penitentiary ones, and you didn't have to look like Osama Bin Laden to feel the brunt of American anger and pain. Like I wasn't hurting as well.

Days became weeks, weeks turned into months, and years followed. Then I went to segregation, back-to-back-to-back for a bunch of carceral bullshit that I don't care to explain. I'm just setting the scene for the lesson at hand.

When you get caught up in a continuous cipher of general population to segregation and back again, you miss out on going to commissary at both ends of the spectrum.

Here I am, after being trapped in that vacuum-like cycle for five months straight sitting in seg once again, waiting for a shower with a piece of Irish Spring soap no thicker than a slice of American cheese.

I prayed to my Guardian Lord as sincerely as a man inside a rowboat lost at sea during a violent storm, "Oh Allah, this is my last piece of soap, and I have to wait at least twenty-one days before seg shops. Please, please, I need some soap."

About ten minutes passed, and a shackled inmate walked by with an escorting officer.

"Hey Rasheed!" yelled the man who had just strolled by from his cell.

"What's up?"

"You straight down there?"

"Yeah, I'm good."

"Man you don't even know who I am, do you?"

"Naw, I don't remember you."

The stranger laughed at my response.

"Man you need something down there?"

"Hell yeah, I need some soap."

"I got you man! It'll be on your bunk when you come from the shower."

I didn't know him, so I took what he said with a grain of salt. But lo and behold, when I returned, there were four fresh bars of Irish Spring on my bed.

"Alhamdulillah!" I screamed out.

Then my Spidey senses got to tingling 'cause I ain't know this dude. So I yelled out, "Hey cuzo, gratitude on the soap, but why you looking out for me?"

He laughed again and said, "Calm down man. I remember when you used to work in the commissary, and I forgot a few items a couple of times, you always went and grabbed the shit for me, and anybody else who needed assistance. You're a real nigga. Let me know if you need something else."

"Good looking."

"All right Sheed."

Personal application analysis

Biblical Economics: "You Reap What You Sow." By using my commissary job as an avenue to help my incarcerated comrades (rule 11), I made a penitentiary friend who held me down when I needed him the most.

RULE 12

Find God

I say this without any fear or reservations—I'm Muslim. I believe in Allah, and I follow the teachings of the Prophet Muhammad Ibn Abdullah of over 1,400 years ago.

Islam teaches me to respect all religion because God is in everything and everyone. And it is my duty as a slave/servant of Allah to call you to the Sirat al-Mustaqim (straight path).

So please do not buy into the subjugation of women, suicide bombings, or any of the numerous misconceived notions displayed through various forms of media and news outlets.

For instance, why would I want my wife to be illiterate when the mother is the first teacher of the child? Unless I want my babies to be stupid. And why would I individually and collectively support a systematically sexist belief system? Nowhere inside the Holy Quran or Sunnah will you ever find anything remotely close to saying, "My wife and daughter should not receive an education because they were born with the wrong genitalia."

That's propaganda, anti-Islamic rhetoric, cultural nonsense, and flat-out falsehood. But don't take my word for it. I invite you to read the Holy Quran and see for yourself because "Nay, we hurl the truth against falsehood, and it knocks out its brain, and behold falsehood doth perish!" (Holy Quran Chapter 21 Verse 18, translated by Abdullah Yusuf Ali).

Without neglecting my duty and staying within the ultimate theme of this book (surviving prison), I am here to tell you about two little-big words that could mean the difference between safety or abuse inside the clink: FIND GOD.

I prefer you to gravitate toward Al-Islam while boxed in. But I'm biased. So with that said, pick a religion that provides you with the best understanding of God, life, and nature. You have a smorgasbord of belief systems to choose from: Black Hebrew Israelites, Buddhism, Catholicism, Christianity, Jehovah's Witnesses, Judaism, Moorish Americans, Nations of Gods and Earth, Nation of Islam, Odinism, Satanism, etcetera.

I beseech you to *find God*, sincerely believe, and follow the tenets of your newfound faith to the best of your abilities. God willing, you'll evolve into a better, stronger, wiser version of yourself. Or at the very least you'll appear to be a true believer, and the covering of your religious brethren will keep you warm and safe throughout the entire institution.

But choose wisely. By comparison, some denominations have more predatory-minded disciples than others.

In addition, be on the lookout for internal beefs within the ranks of your faith. If one exists, never pick a side and always take the high road.

To illustrate, let's say you've just been baptized and you accept Jesus Christ as your personal Lord and Savior. Now that you are no longer on the outside looking in, you begin to build closer relationships with your Christian brethren. You quickly learn that the congregation is divided on a particular ideology. One side believes that blah-blah-blah should be implemented. And the others wanna teach the yada-yada-yada doctrine.

Do not pick a side. I repeat, do not pick a side, even if the totality of facts supports one group over the other. Simply say, "What would Jesus do?" And leave it at that. Because the only thing worse than a fighter/killer is someone who believes that he's fighting/killing in the name of God, believe that!

Sometimes in jail, serving God gets a bad rap. You're going to hear a lot of inmates speaking out the side of their necks like, "I hate guys who come to jail and find religion. Why you ain't find God in the world?" "Them niggas just scared of prison so they running to God for help." "That coward just looking for protection."

And on and on.

There may be a multitude of reasons why these men spew such words of contempt. But the fact of the matter is they are telling you through their heated opinions how finding God in prison provides shelter.

Your safekeeping stems from the congregation. A nice percentage of ex-gang chiefs sincerely find God. Even though these leaders may have retired or stepped away from the gang life, the little homies still look out for them and value their opinions. So you may be praising God right next to a made man and not even know it. If you are a sincere believer or appear to be one, all he has to do is lightheartedly mention that you're okay, and the little homies will give you a pass.

Equally, your church also consists of extremely violent street dudes who have wholeheartedly given their life over to God. The guys who knew these superdangerous thugs before their conversion are secretly praying to the "powers that be" to please keep these men inside the house of God. So don't you ever think that you don't have any assistance if a problem arises. Meekness is not weakness; it's strength under control. So best believe Brother John is more brutal than two life-sized Chucky dolls put together. Find God!

Personal application of rule 12

I was one of those semidangerous dudes who found God (rule 12) in prison, Alhamdulillah. I plugged in with like minds and quickly discovered that "The Believers, men and women, are protectors, one of another" (Holy Quran Chapter 9 Verse 71 translated by Abdullah Yusuf Ali).

Personal application analysis

In the penitentiary, all religions have a made man or two and a multitude of reformed violent thugs. The only thing that is required for shelter is sincere belief, or fake it till you make it outside the institutional walls.

Closing Note

A swimming instructor is not someone who knows the physics of how solids behave in liquids, but s/he can give lessons on how to swim. In a similar manner, I can't begin to tell you why carceral violence is so rampant amid Illinois's county jails and penal institutions, but I can teach you how to survive.

In closing, my twelve rules of survival are like a penitentiary GPS system designed to guide you safely back through the doors of freedom.

Take heed…

Take heed…

You're welcome.

Glossary

Allah. The Creator of the heavens and earth

ASAP. An acronym for "as soon as possible"

back to back. To place your back upon another man's back and defend yourselves from opposing violence

banger. An engineered penitentiary knife

beat down. To be physically assaulted

belled. To run away

bid. The amount of time spent in prison

books. The place where the correctional center holds your outside money; also known as an Inmate Trust Fund Account

bopper. Slang for police or correctional officers

boxed in. To be incarcerated or trapped in a jail cell

bro. Short for brother

buck up. Stand up like a man to face a difficult situation

bump heads. To have a verbal and/or physical confrontation with someone else

bussed down. To open up your booty hole

carry. The amount of time you will have to serve in a prison, if convicted for a specific offence

catch a body. To be charged and arraigned for murder

cellie. A jailhouse roommate

charge. An offense that is punishable by probation, parole, or jail time

choppin' it up. To reminisce on old times with a friend or to have a conversation

click. A group of homies, gang members, or friends

come get it like Tyson. A slick way of saying it's time to fight fast, hard, and violent like Mike Tyson

commissary. A penitentiary grocery store where inmates can purchase clothing, electronics, food, and hygiene items

contraband. Illegal or prohibited items

copper. Slang for police or correctional officer

correctional sex. Prison homosexual lovemaking

count-check to count-check. Set times throughout the day when correctional staff counts the inmate population to ensure that all incarcerated men are alive and present (e.g., 7:00 a.m. to 3:00 p.m.)

creased. Split or cut down the middle

crew. A group of homies, gang members, or friends

dead broke. To have no money or insufficient funds

deck. A confined common area where inmates eat, shit, sleep, and shower

deck go up. A riot or gang fight inside an inmate commons area

deep at. To have more gang members than a rival group

DMX. A gangster rap artist, hood poet

duke shoot. A booty hole

Eukanuba. An inexpensive dog food

faggotry. Homosexual activities

finta. "Going to" or "I am about to"

fleek. The latest style, what's hot, or fashionable

flicks. Digital photos, selfies, or pictures

fo. "For"

fun boys. Male homosexuals

gallery. Prison slang for the floor level that your cell is located

game. Knowledge, hood intellect, or reasoning skills

gang. An abundance or a lot

gangster swag. An attitude or smooth disposition

gas station food. The cakes, cookies, or pops sold at the inmate commissary

gear. Your clothing, shoes, or apparel

geeche. A homosexual man

get at you. To want to fight or do bodily harm

gilla. Another word for game or knowledge

give you a pass. To forgive you of an incident or to not bother you

good looking. A slick way of saying thank you

gone. To get out the way

Grey Goose. An institutional bus designed to transport inmates

had words. To have a verbal confrontation with someone

he did that. He got away with something

held me down. To assist someone mentally, spiritually, physically, or
    financially

hoe bath. To bathe in a bathroom sink like a low-class prostitute

holler. To talk to

homie-homie. A brother and friend

homo-thug. A street thug that is a homosexual

hooked up. In a gang or affiliated

hots. Prison slang for a state-issued prison meal

huff. Some bogus weed

hut. A prison cell

I'm a. Short for "I am about to"

Inmate Trust Fund Account. An institutional account that holds an
    inmate's outside money for commissary purchases

in the door. The first thing you did or an initial move

in-violation. To be physically punished by your gang organization

ism. Game, information, or knowledge

joint. Prison or correctional facility

juice. To have gang status or respect

jugging. To crack jokes or make fun of someone

kool-points. Actions that determine your level of acceptance from
    your peers

li'l respecties. Respect

lit. Short for gang literature

literature. Gang laws and bylaws

lootchie. Money, cash, or dinero

L7. A square, lame, or not-so-cool person

made man. Someone who has rank or receives major respect from
    his peers

merch. Short for merchandise

mix it up. To fight

mob. Homies, gang partners, or friends

money vouchers. An institutional slip utilized by an inmate to send money from his trust fund account

Ms. Butterface. Everything look good but her face

mugged up. To purposely look angry, mad, or upset

my bag. "Pardon me" or "excuse me"

neutrons. Incarcerated men who are not in a gang

one gone. To lose something

one-eighty. To turn around and face the other way; to change the direction of your life

on the new. Someone new to the prison system or a specific penal situation

opposition. Rival gangs

Orange Crush. The penitentiary emergence response team members

paperwork. Slang for gang literature

pass 'em. To move past

peeped. To see or observe something

peoples. My family members, homies, and friends

peoples get at you. Revenge or a violent act

penitentiary friend. A bond formed in prison

penitentiary sling. To be beaten so badly that you need medical assistance

Pimpin' Ken. A world-renowned pimp

pimpin' pimpin'. A nickname for smooth or laidback individuals

pimpish. To act like a pimp

pod. The confined common area where inmates eat, shit, sleep, and shower

po-po. Slang for the police

pokey. A correctional center

police-ism. The things that the authorities do to maintain control

popped off. To start or begin

push comes to shove. If one is forced to do something

punk. A homosexual or mistreat

rat. A tattletale, stool pigeon, or snitch

rego weed. Regular, naturally grown marijuana

riding dirty. Willfully indulging in something illegal

run. An attempt to control

R2-D2. A popular android from hit movie series *Star Wars*

seg. Short for segregation

setting out. Unlawful human sex trafficking

set you out. To bring an undercover stool pigeon to light

shady. To do something dirty, sneaky, or deceptive

shakedown. When a correctional officer searches an inmate's cell for contraband

sham. A trick or something phony

somebody got to get it. Someone has to be physically punished for the incident at hand

speaking ill. To talk negatively about something or someone

speaking out of turn. Having a comment or talking about an issue that is none of your business

speaking out the side of your neck. To gossip or to talk crazy

Spidey senses. An innate feeling that something bad is about to happen

spork. A spoon and a fork combined together as one

squared off. Before the physical altercation begins, two individuals throw their guards up for protection

stand down. To not get involved in other people's affairs; tend to your own business

state tray. An institutional meal offered for breakfast, lunch, and dinner

stint. The amount of time spent in prison

stole. To punch an unsuspecting person in the face

stuck. To stab someone with a knife

stupid fat. An abundance, big, or a lot

swoll. Muscular or strong-looking; swollen

swolled. Bigger than normal; massive

sword. A knife

T. Short for T-shirt

tearing off. To forcibly rape someone

tear this bitch up. To start a riot or gang fight

thang. Thing

the whole shebang. Everything

THOT. An acronym for "that hoe out there"

took the joint back. When the prison administration took back
control of their facilities from the inmate population

treated. To be disrespected or taken advantage of

trigger words. Words that cause you to react violently

try you. To test your resolve

twist. A slick word for police or correctional officer

two for one. To borrow an item in prison and repay two

violation. To be physically assaulted or to break a rule

write-out. A prestamped envelope used for mailing letters

yo. Short for you, your, or you are

you feel me? "Do you understand?"

402 Conference. A situation where people talk a problem out instead
of getting physical

About the Author

After 26 Years Straight of long term Incarceration, Raylan Gilford ID # B-66509 has evolved into a self-appointed penitentiary specialist, who holds a master's degree in Prison Psychology and a PhD in carceral survival.

Acquisition of such lofty-traumatic degree's, Hail from Illinois World Renowned Penal Universities; Where the wrong move could cost you your sanity, or even worst, your life.

Mr. Gilford cleverly uses His Carceral experience of Pain and Misfortune not only to Shed a 400 Watt light Bulb upon the daily injustices of the prison system, but to also bring Hyper-Awareness to the trauma every incarcerated citizen succumb to, at one point in time, or another. A syndrome which he has rightly labeled progressive traumatic prison stress syndrome (PTPSS).

Raylan Currently resides at Danville Correctional Center and will be released in the near future.

Printed in the USA
CPSIA information can be obtained
at www.ICGtesting.com
LVHW051028120823
755047LV00039B/462